Tidbits
on
Tennessee Family Law

Your Introduction to Tennessee Family Law

Princess M. Woodard, Esq.

RIVERHOUSE PUBLISHING, LLC
MEMPHIS

RH
RIVERHOUSE
PUBLISHING

Tidbits on Tennessee Family Law:
Your Introduction to Tennessee Family Law

RiverHouse Publishing, LLC
65 Germantown Court
Suite 200
Cordova, TN 38018

ISBN: 978-1-7335622-6-3

www.woodardesq.com
www.riverhousepublishingllc.com

Table of Contents

Disclaimer

The law is ever evolving, and each case is different. This book is an introduction to Tennessee family law and is neither all-encompassing nor intended to replace legal representation. The content of this book is for informational purposes only and is not intended to serve as legal authority. In purchasing or reading this book, you understand this book is not intended as a substitute for consultation with a licensed attorney. The purchasing or reading of this book does not establish an attorney-client relationship with the author. Please consult with an attorney to discuss the unique details of your legal issue(s).

The publisher and the author make no guarantees concerning the level of success you may experience by following the advice and strategies contained in this book, and you accept the risk that results will differ for everyone. The case illustrations and examples provided in this book show exceptional results, which may not apply to your case, and are not intended to represent or guarantee you will achieve the same or similar results.

Although the publisher and the author have tried to ensure that the information in this book was correct at press time and while this publication provides accurate information regarding the subject covered, the publisher and the author assume no responsibility for errors, inaccuracies, omissions, or any other inconsistencies herein and disclaim any liability to any party for any loss, damage, or disruption caused by errors or omissions, whether such errors or omissions result from negligence, accident, or any other cause.

Introduction

Lawyers often forget that the average person knows nothing about divorce, child support, visitation, or any other family law issue and their introduction to it is when they are smack dab in the middle of a legal dispute. Family law matters are often emotional, stressful, and scary. Processing the breakdown of a marriage while litigating a divorce or mourning the death of a child when fighting for custody of a grandchild can be overwhelming and a difficult process to navigate, especially with scarce knowledge.

I wrote this book because I asked myself, "If you weren't an attorney, what would you know about divorce law, child support law, paternal rights, adoption, etc.?" and my answer to myself was "Nothing or very little." I then asked myself, "What would I want to know?" When representing a client, my goal is to always provide them with the knowledge they need to understand their case and make informed decisions. Often people's logic and the law don't agree. This book was birthed out of my belief that knowledge is power.

This book is your uncomplicated introduction to family law in Tennessee and is intended to be a resource for anyone willingly or unwillingly entering the arena of family law. *Tidbits on Tennessee Family Law* is certain to dispel common misconceptions, provide insightful knowledge, and serve as a helpful navigation tool.

Chapter 1:
Parentage and Paternity

Tennessee law on parentage is not that different from other states but is often not what the average person would think if they were asked how parentage, for the purpose of parental rights, is established. Know that with the law, legal requirements differ depending on the legal issue; for example, the legal requirements for establishing paternity so a child may inherit from their father differ from the legal requirements to establish parentage and paternal rights for a father in a custody matter. According to the Centers for Disease Control and Prevention, 44 percent of Tennessee children born in 2019 were born to unmarried mothers. As maternity is often not disputable, mothers have sole custody of children born out of wedlock and fathers must take legal action to invoke their parental rights. This chapter will discuss the legal steps fathers must take to establish their legal rights. This chapter will also discuss a Tennessee law regarding children born to married women, which often leaves people scratching their heads. Throughout this chapter, we will explore when and how parentage is established, how parentage is handled for married persons, and why, when, and how paternity may be disestablished. For this book, parentage and paternity are often used interchangeably, but parentage may refer to the mother or father while paternity refers exclusively to the father.

A.
Children Born to a Married Woman

Children born to a married woman are legally presumed to be the natural children of the woman's husband even if the parties are physically separated.[1] This presumption also applies to marriages that may be deemed illegal, void, or voidable (which are usually dissolved by annulment). This presumption also survives death, and therefore a child may inherit from the mother's husband unless paternity is disestablished (which may be accomplished via paternity testing of the biological father or genetic testing between the child and a blood relative of the deceased husband).[2]

The husband/presumptive father will have all legal rights and obligations toward the child until paternity is disestablished. Child support may be established against the husband/presumptive father until paternity is disestablished, and any child support owed by him that went unpaid before disestablishment will still be owed even after disestablishment; disestablishing paternity for a husband/presumptive father will terminate only ongoing child support and prevent pursuit of future child support. While parentage and paternity for unmarried parents are handled by juvenile court,[3] divorce courts have jurisdic-

---

[1] A rebuttable presumption; Tennessee Code § 36-2-304 (2021).

[2] Disestablishment means a court has held that the husband is not the legal father of the child.

[3] Juvenile Court or the court in the county that hears legal cases concerning children born out of wedlock.

tion over parentage for married couples; therefore, disestablishment for the husband/presumptive father must be handled in divorce court. However, juvenile court may establish paternity for the biological father if it is not disclosed to the court that the mother is married and the child was born during her marriage. If the court is informed that the child was born while mother was married to someone else, juvenile court will require disestablishment of the child via the divorce court before establishing paternity in juvenile court for the biological father.

If a separated couple went to juvenile court to address child support for their children and it was disclosed that the wife has had a child during the marriage by a third party, the husband's child support order will include a child support obligation for that non-biological child until the couple or either party seeks disestablishment of paternity through the divorce court. As discussed later in this book, juvenile court and divorce courts have concurrent jurisdiction over child support for separated married couples, and child support may be established even if a married couple has not filed for divorce, if they are living separately.

The legal presumption of parentage for the husband must be disestablished by a court. The party seeking to disestablish paternity must either submit to the court paternity testing excluding the husband as the biological father, paternity testing establishing someone else as the biological father, or an order from another court establishing someone else as the legal father.[4]

---

[4] This may occur in a paternity related juvenile court case in which there was no disclosure that the child was born while the mother was married to someone other than the biological father.

In some divorces, neither the husband/presumptive father nor the wife will seek to disestablish paternity of a child, not naturally the husband's but born during the marriage, if the husband has established a paternal relationship with the child and the parties seek to maintain that paternal relationship post-divorce. In those cases, the child is treated like a biological child of the parties and the court will not force disestablishment. A husband/presumptive father that is aware at the time of divorcing that he is not the biological father but waives or declines disestablishment upon finalization of the divorce cannot seek to disestablish paternity post-divorce. If at the time of divorce, the husband cannot pursue paternity disestablishment because the wife and children's whereabouts are unknown,[5] he must notify the court of his assertion that he is not the biological father of children born to his wife since the date of marriage. In this scenario, the husband will remain the presumptive father of the children until paternity testing may be conducted; the court will reserve paternity disestablishment until that time.

Children born to a married man by a woman other than his wife are addressed as children born to unmarried parents; there is no legal presumption. A man who fathers a child with a married woman who is not his spouse must file for paternity with the court to establish himself as the biological father of the child and to establish his legal paternal rights. However, there may be limitations in the biological father establishing paternity for the child and he may be forced to wait until the mother divorces her husband and hope that the divorcing couple addresses paternity disestablishment during the divorce. In

[5] Divorce granted by default judgment, see Chapter 5.

Tennessee, if the mother/wife remains married and co-habits with her husband during the period of conception, pregnancy, and birth of the child, the biological father has only twelve months from the child's birth to file a paternity petition.

B.
Children Born to a Divorced Woman Within 300 Days of Finalization of Divorce

Children born to a divorced woman within 300 days of finalization of divorce are also legally presumed to be the natural children of the woman's now ex-husband and paternity must be disestablished. This presumption also applies to marriages deemed illegal, void, or voidable (usually dissolved via annulment). The best course of action, if available, is to have parentage disestablished during the divorce proceedings. If it is known during the pendency of the divorce that the wife is pregnant by a third party or has had a child by a third party, paternity testing must be completed before the finalization of divorce.[6] If the ex-husband learns of the ex-wife's pregnancy or that she has given birth to a child within 300 days of the divorce, he must file a petition to disestablish paternity with the divorce court to ensure that his legal presumption of parentage is extinguished. The ex-husband's presumption of parentage may also be disestablished via a paternity or child support case involving the ex-wife and the child's biological father; however, if it is disclosed via the paternity or child support case that the child was born within 300 days of the mother's divorce, the divorce case will need to be reopened to properly disestablish the

[6] This does not apply in cases in which the wife is pregnant by a third party for the benefit of the marriage (i.e., sperm donor), as those children will be treated as a child of the marriage.

ex-husband as the presumptive father. This is a common scenario when the married couple divorced before the wife learned of her pregnancy, the wife concealed her pregnancy, or the husband obtained a divorce from his wife by default judgment.

Divorce courts will often ask if the wife is pregnant during the final divorce proceedings to ensure there will not be a post-divorce paternity issue.[7] For women pregnant by someone other than their husband, prenatal paternity testing must be presented to the court to finalize the divorce before the child's birth. If prenatal paternity testing is not an option for the parties, then the divorce will not be finalized until the child is born and paternity testing is conducted.

To avoid the cost of paternity testing, some divorcing spouses conceal that the wife has had a child by a third party during the marriage or is pregnant by a third party. This information should always be disclosed to the court, as the financial consequences and judicial reprimand, including the husband being barred from later seeking disestablishment if he knowingly participated in the concealment, will far exceed the costs associated with testing.

---

[7] Pregnancy is not a basis to prevent or delay the filing of a divorce.

C.
Children Born to Unmarried Parents

The only presumption regarding paternity for men to children born to unmarried parents is created when the father executes a Voluntary Acknowledgment of Paternity.[8] A Voluntary Acknowledgment of Paternity may be completed at birth or any time after the child's birth. The signing father's name will be listed on the child's birth certificate following execution of the Voluntary Acknowledgment of Paternity. Signing a Voluntary Acknowledgement of Paternity shall constitute a legal finding of paternity for the signing father. The child who is the subject of the signed Voluntary Acknowledgment of Paternity is for all purposes the legal child of the signing father; however, the invoking of parental rights for the signing father requires court action. Mothers have sole legal and physical custody of children born to unmarried parents until legal action is taken.

A paternity suit may be brought by the mother, father, the state, or a caregiver.[9] A paternity suit will establish the legal father and may provide the father with some paternal rights, including joint legal custody;[10] however, additional legal action is often required to seek

[8] Tennessee Code § 24-7-113 (2021).

[9] A caregiver is a relative or non-relative who has legal temporary or permanent custody of the child but has not adopted the child.

[10] Joint legal custody means that both parents have the same parental rights, but physical custody and parenting time are addressed separately.

custody and/or visitation rights, invoke the "parental bill of rights," and trigger other parental statutes (discussed more in Chapter 3). At a paternity hearing, parties may agree that the alleged father is the biological father and the court may waive paternity testing. If there is no agreement between the parties and the alleged father has not executed a Voluntary Acknowledgment of Paternity, the court will order paternity testing.

The court will not require paternity testing if the alleged father has completed a Voluntary Acknowledgment of Paternity; however, the father may request paternity testing if he has a basis to contest paternity (examples include statements of the mother, a third party claiming to be the father, et cetera). The court may take a default judgment for paternity against a father who signed a Voluntary Acknowledgment of Paternity which could result in a child support obligation being established against the father without his attendance at the hearing.[11] Challenging paternity after execution of a Voluntary Acknowledgment of Paternity is time-sensitive; therefore, if a father is concerned about paternity, DNA testing should be conducted before completion a Voluntary Acknowledgment of Paternity.

---

[11] A default judgment is defined as the court granting the plaintiff/petitioner permission to proceed in a legal action without the consent or participation of the defendant/respondent if the defendant/respondent was properly served, via personal service or publication, and has failed to respond or participate; Paternity petitions are usually filed to initiate child support proceedings.

Typically, paternity suits will automatically trigger the establishment of child support, even absent a specific request for financial support.

Bonus Tidbit: A petition to establish paternity may be filed after the death of the alleged father; the petition may be brought by the mother or the estate of the deceased alleged father. DNA testing of a close relative of the alleged father, typically a parent of the alleged father, will be required.

Bonus Tidbit: At the time of this book's publication, a bill is pending in the Tennessee General Assembly that would require paternity testing before the signing of a child's birth certificate is legally binding to establish paternity against an unwed father.

D.
Disestablishing Paternity for Unmarried Parents

Disestablishing paternity after execution of a Voluntary Acknowledgment of Paternity may be accomplished in one of two ways. Where a Voluntary Acknowledgment of Paternity is executed, a Rescission of Voluntary Acknowledgment of Paternity may be submitted to the Tennessee Vital Records Office within sixty days of completing the Voluntary Acknowledgment of Paternity. For cases that do not qualify for submission of a Rescission of the Voluntary Acknowledgment of Paternity, a petition to disestablish paternity must be filed with the juvenile court or the court in the county overseeing legal matters involving children born out of wedlock. The petition to disestablish paternity must allege fraud, duress, or material mistake of fact and the party seeking disestablishment must prove to the court that the Voluntary Acknowledgment of Paternity was executed due to fraud, duress, or material mistake of fact. If the court finds fraud, duress, or material mistake of fact related to the father's execution of the Voluntary Acknowledgment of Paternity then paternity testing will be ordered and upon results excluding the assumed father, paternity will be disestablished, and he will be removed from the child's birth certificate.

In Tennessee, the statute of limitations to disestablish parentage was five years from the initial acknowledgment of paternity;[12] however, a petition to disestablish paternity was not be barred by the statute of limitations if fraud in the procurement by the mother of the child was found and disestablishment would not affect the interests of the child, the state, or any Title IV-D agency.[13] Fraud in the procurement is simply defined as using deliberate deception to obtain the father's acknowledgment of paternity. Fraud in the procurement usually occurs where the mother knowingly misrepresented paternity to the alleged father to have him sign the child's birth certificate or execute a Voluntary Acknowledgment of Paternity. The court could deny disestablishment, even after finding fraud in the procurement and paternity testing excluding the alleged father, if it determined disestablishment would hurt the interest of the child, the state, or any Title IV-D agency, which is limited to cases in which a meaningful parent-child relationship had been established, or disestablishment could have resulted in the child being parentless or becoming a ward of the state.

Effective July 1, 2022, the disestablishment of paternity law has been amended to eliminate the five-year statute of limitation and the requirement of fraud in the procurement after five years. After July 1, 2022, a petition to disestablish paternity may be filed at any time on the grounds of fraud, duress, or material mistake of fact. *Tennessee HB 2699; Tennessee SB 1779*

---

[12] This does not apply to cases in which parentage was automatically established against the mother's husband.

[13] Title IV-D agencies are all state agencies administrating child support enforcement plans approved under Title IV-D of the Social Security Act and other interested individuals.

Chapter 2:
Child Support

There is a frequent public argument about which expenses should be paid with child support money. The purpose of child support is to help with the day-to-day care of a child while the child is in the care of someone other than the parent paying child support.

The person receiving child support may use the funds in any way necessary to ensure the child's basic daily needs are met, which may include housing expenses (i.e., rent or mortgage), transportation expenses (i.e., the payee's car note or gas costs), and household expenses (i.e., utilities, cable, internet, and household supplies). No rule requires child support to be used on direct expenses of the child (i.e., clothes, food only for the child, or the child's activities). The parent paying child support is responsible for contributing to the daily needs of the child when the child is not in their personal care; therefore, the paying parent pays less or more in child support depending upon how much time the child is in their personal care. In Tennessee, ongoing child support ends when the child turns eighteen and graduates from high school;[14] however, child support will continue for adult children with special needs until the age of 21 and, depending on the severity of the needs, may continue beyond the age of 21 or permanently.

---

[14] If the child fails to graduate, then it is when the child's class graduates.

There is a lot of misinformation surrounding child support. This chapter will discuss when child support is established, what factors are considered when calculating child support, and will share child support facts to help eliminate the misinformation surrounding this hot-button topic.

A.
When Child Support is Established by the Court

An unmarried parent, a physically separated married parent, the state, or a caregiver may file to establish child support. Child support is automatically addressed in divorces with minor children and disabled adult children. The state is only involved in child support cases in which Title IV-D services are involved. For unmarried parents, juvenile court has exclusive jurisdiction over child support, and child support is established when a petition for parentage or petition for child support is filed with the court.[15] If the alleged father has signed the birth certificate or a Voluntary Acknowledgment of Paternity, then only a petition to establish child support is needed and the father must dispute paternity, as we discussed in Chapter 1. If the alleged father has not acknowledged paternity, then parentage must be established before child support can be addressed and DNA testing will be conducted unless expressly waived by the alleged father.[16]

Juvenile Court also shares jurisdiction with divorce courts for child support cases involving married and divorced couples. If a married couple is living separately, child support may be pursued and ordered in juvenile court even though the parties have not filed to dissolve the marriage. Child support will remain in juvenile court

---

[15] Juvenile Court or the court in the county that hears cases involving children born out of wedlock.

[16] Alleged fathers should always request DNA testing.

even after the parties file to dissolve the marriage.[17] If at the time of filing for divorce, child support has not been filed for or ordered by juvenile court, the divorce court will order child support as part of the divorce finalization. Child support cannot be ordered for married parties living together. For divorcing couples, child support cannot be waived and must be addressed as part of the dissolution of the marriage (divorce, legal separation, or annulment). Temporary child support may also be requested and ordered by the divorce court, if the parties are living separately, while a divorce is pending. If juvenile court has jurisdiction over child support, the divorce court cannot modify the child support order; the parties must seek modifications through juvenile court.

Even though child support cases cannot be transferred from juvenile court to the divorce court, the issue of child support will be transferred from the divorce court to juvenile court if Title IV-D services are involved.[18] Title IV-D services are triggered upon receipt of certain government benefits or upon the request of the payee parent for the state to pursue and/or enforce child support. Some payee parents will request Title IV-D services because the state has greater resources to employ more child support enforcement efforts and options, such as intercepting tax refunds and filing for contempt against the payor parent due to nonpayment. For cases involving Title IV-D services, the state may file a petition for support and the parties cannot object to nor waive child support.[19] For child support cases not

---

[17] Divorce, legal separation, or annulment.

[18] State-run child support enforcement programs and for receipt of certain government benefits by the custodial parent.

[19] If IV-D services are involved, child support will be established in cases of unmarried parents even if they are living together. Child support will terminate only

involving Title IV-D services and for private direct pay cases,[20] the payee is responsible for seeking certain relief, such as intercepting tax return funds and filing for contempt due to nonpayment. In child support cases not involving Title IV-D services, child support can still be processed through Tennessee's Disbursement Unit and the court ordering child support can issue income withholding orders to the payor's employer.

Caregivers have the legal right to file for child support and may request child support against either parent or both parents. Caregivers must have a court order giving them custody, temporarily or permanently, to pursue child support. Parents ordered to pay child support to a caregiver should always request that the court allot income to the other parent if the other parent is not involved in the case when calculating child support owed to the caregiver. This is important because the payor parent's obligation is likely to be higher if no income is assigned to the other parent.

---

if the parties marry each other, or in limited cases if the payee parent terminates IV-D services (this is generally limited to cases in which the payee requested IV-D services and does not apply to cases in which the payee parent or child received certain government benefits).

[20] A case in which support is not filtered through the child support receipting office but being paid directly (i.e., check, money order, cash, and wire transfer) to the payee parent from the payor parent. While the child support is paid directly to the payee parent, the child support amount and order are established by the court.

B.
What is Considered Income for the Purposes of Calculating Child Support?

Child support is calculated using the parents' gross incomes, with adjustments made for self-employed taxes being paid by either parent and any Social Security or Veterans benefit paid to the child on a parent's account. For caregiver cases, no income is assessed to the caregiver when calculating child support. The Tennessee Child Support Guidelines identify gross income as income realized from any of the following sources:[21]

- Wages
- Salaries
- Commissions, fees, and tips
- Income from self-employment less reasonable and necessary expenses required to produce such income (example: fuel for a trucker driver, a rental property's mortgage for a landlord, or materials for a manufacturer)
- Bonuses
- Overtime payments
- Severance pay

[21] Rules of Tennessee Department of Human Services Child Support Services Division, Chapter 1240-02-04-.04; Child Support Guidelines.

- Pensions or retirement plans including, but not limited to, those from Social Security, Veterans Affairs Department, Railroad Retirement Board, Keogh plans, and Individual Retirement Accounts (IRAs)
- Interest income
- Dividend income
- Trust income
- Annuities
- Net capital gains
- Disability or retirement benefits received from the Social Security Administration under Title II of the Social Security Act or from the Veterans Affairs Department, whether paid to the parent or to the child based upon the parent's account (If the benefit is paid directly to the child, there is a designated column on the child support worksheet and calculator to list the monthly benefit amount)
- Workers' compensation benefits, whether temporary or permanent
- Unemployment insurance benefits
- Judgments recovered for personal injuries and awards from other civil actions
- Gifts that consist of cash or other liquid instruments, or which can be converted to cash, or which can produce income such as real estate, or which reduce a parent's living expenses such as housing paid by others, in whole or in part
- Inheritances that consist of cash or other liquid instruments, or which can be converted to cash, or which can produce income, such as real estate
- Prizes
- Lottery winnings

- Alimony or maintenance received from persons other than parties to the proceeding before the court
- Actual income earned during incarceration by an inmate

For self-employed parents, child support is calculated using their gross income after deducting for business expenses necessary to generate the income. There are also deductions that a self-employed parent may claim on their tax returns that the court will add back into the parent's income. Those deductions include depreciation,[22] personal vehicle expenses, and cell phone services if the phone is used for personal and business calls.

Bonus Tidbit: For self-employed parents, declarations and statements of income may be used to establish and/or impute the income for the self-employed parent. Examples of declarations and statements of income include income disclosures made on loan applications, financial statements, lease and rental applications, and credit card applications. Banking activity, statements, and deposit history may also be used to establish and/or impute the income for a self-employed parent.

---

[22] There are a few limited exceptions, but customarily any amount listed on a Schedule C of the 1040 federal tax return as depreciation will be added back into the self-employed parent's income. A Schedule C is used to state the income or loss and deductions of a sole proprietorship business or profession.

C.
Unemployed and Underemployed Parents

For unemployed parents not receiving money from any of the previously listed sources, the court will determine if the parent is voluntarily unemployed and impute the parent's income based on a variety of factors. Income will also be imputed for parents determined to be voluntarily underemployed and parents who own substantial non-income-producing assets such as vacant land, collectibles, and non-rental properties.

The lowest monthly income that will be imputed to a parent is either poverty level, which is between $900 and $1,000 per month, or minimum wage, at $1,200 to $1,300 per month. Imputation to poverty level or minimum wage is generally reserved for parents with limited education, skills, work history, and/or physical capacity. "The Court first turns to a parent's present and past work history, education, training, and ability to work in determining what amount the parent's monthly income should be imputed to. A parent's extravagant lifestyle, including ownership of valuable assets and resources may also be considered when imputing income".[23] The rise of social media has led to the social media content of the payor parent being used as evidence to establish the lifestyle and income of the payor parent.

---

[23] Rules of Tennessee Department of Human Services Child Support Services Division, Chapter 1240-02-04- .04; Child Support Guidelines.

This is common where a parent is self-employed or claiming that they are unemployed.[24]

Stay-at-home parents are given special consideration, and the basis of imputing income for stay-at-home parents is based upon three factors: 1) Whether the parent acted in the role of full-time caretaker while the parents were living in the same household, 2) The time the parent staying at home has remained out of the workforce for the purpose of being a caregiver, and 3) The age of the minor child(ren).

If a parent fails or refuses to produce adequate or reliable proof of income and the court cannot determine the parent's income or earning potential, then the court must consider, but is not limited to, the following factors:[25]

- Assets
- Residence
- Employment and earnings history
- Job skills
- Educational attainment
- Literacy
- Age
- Health
- Criminal record and other employment barriers
- Records of seeking work
- The local job market
- The availability of employers willing to hire the parent

---

[24] The opposing party or their attorney may present to the court the social media posts and activities of the payor parent during the support hearing.

[25] Rules of Tennessee Department of Human Services Child Support Services Division, Chapter 1240-02-04- .04; Child Support Guidelines.

- Prevailing earnings level in the local community
- Other relevant background factors

"If there is no adequate and reliable evidence of current income and imputation of income is authorized, gross income for the current and prior years shall be determined by imputing annual gross income of forty-three thousand seven hundred sixty-one dollars ($43,761) for male parents and thirty-five thousand nine hundred thirty-six dollars ($35,936) for female parents. These figures represent the full-time, year-round workers' median gross income, for the Tennessee population only, from the American Community Survey of 2016 from the U.S. Census Bureau".[26] Income may be imputed to a higher or lesser amount depending upon the particular facts of a case. An example would be imputing the mother's income to $3,000 per month based upon the unemployed mother maintaining and paying monthly bills of $3,000.

An underemployed parent is a parent held by the court to be earning less than their education, skills, and previous employment history establishes they have the ability to earn. Upon the finding that a parent is underemployed, the court may impute the parent's income to a previous income or salary; the court may also impute the income to the median for someone with similar education, skills, or previous employment history. An example of someone being found to be voluntarily underemployed is a father who held special certification and was earning an annual salary of $75,000 from his previous employment, but lost that job due to repeated tardiness and now has a

---

[26] Rules of Tennessee Department of Human Services Child Support Services Division, Chapter 1240-02-04- .04; Child Support Guidelines.

new job in another field with an annual salary of $30,000. The Court has a sufficient basis to find the father voluntarily underemployed, as he lost his previous job due to his own actions and impute his income to $75,000 based upon his previous employment and certification.

D.
Expenses Considered When Calculating Child Support

When calculating child support, parents are entitled to credits for certain expenses, including childcare, health insurance premiums,[27] out-of-pocket recurring medical expenses, documented child support payments that either parent is paying for their other children and for biological or adopted children living in either parent's home. While these expenses must be factored when calculating child support, consideration may also be given to extraordinary educational expenses and special expenses (i.e., summer camp, extracurricular activities, and cultural development activities) which are referred to as deviations. If a deviation is permitted by the court, the payor parent will be ordered to pay a percentage of the deviation expense(s) and that amount will be added to the child support obligation.

[27] Monthly premiums paid by the parent or the parent's spouse.

E.
The Tennessee Child Support Worksheet and Calculator

Child support is calculated by inputting information into the Tennessee Child Support Worksheet and Calculator.[28] Besides the parties and court details, the first information inputted into the worksheet and calculator should be about the child(ren) involved in the pending case, which would include their names, birth dates, and annual parenting time for each parent.

For child support, parenting time is calculated as overnights and periods of twelve or more consecutive hours over the previous twelve months. Denial of parenting time and contempt of visitation orders are addressed separately from child support calculations because child support is based on the actual parenting time exercised. However, courts may consider such factors as the child being employed and having certain schedule commitments if the payor parent has not exercised consistent parenting time with older children.

Second, the parents' incomes, applicable self-employed taxes, and federal benefits received for the child(ren) on the parent's account are put into the worksheet and calculator.[29] Third, credits for childcare, health insurance premiums,[30] and out-of-pocket recurring medical

[28] The Tennessee Child Support Worksheet and Calculator is an electronic multiple page worksheet which calculates child support based upon the state's formula.
[29] Federal benefits include Social Security Disability and Retirement along with Veterans' derivative pay.
[30] Not to exceed 5% of the gross monthly income for the parent providing health insurance coverage.

expenses are input into the worksheet and calculator. Next, in-home biological and adopted children are listed for each parent, followed by documented monthly child support paid by either parent for all other children outside of the pending case.

Last, deviations for any extraordinary educational expenses or special expenses are included. Once all the information is provided, a final child support monthly obligation is calculated. In cases of child support modifications, additional information is listed in the worksheet and calculator, which is addressed later in this chapter.

In 2020, the Tennessee Child Support Guidelines were modified to create a minimum child support obligation of $100 per month unless the payor's only source of income is Supplemental Security Income (SSI), the federal benefit for a child results in a calculation of support owed to be less than the minimum amount, or if the parenting time adjustment results in an amount less than the minimum child support order. The Tennessee Child Support Worksheet and Calculator will automatically calculate the parenting time adjustment's monetary amount.

The Tennessee Child Support Guidelines were updated in 2020 to establish a self-support reserve for payor parents of at least $1,150 per month to ensure they have enough money for basic needs while fulfilling their child support obligations.[31] The self-support reserve means that the court-ordered child support payment cannot result in

---

[31] *Tennessee Revises Child Support Guidelines to Better Serve Families.* (2020, May 11). Tennessee Department of Human Services.
https://www.tn.gov/humanservices/news/2020/5/11/tennessee-revises-child-support-guidelines-to-better-serve-families.html

the payor having less than $1,150 per month to maintain and pay their personal living expenses.

F.
Modification of Child Support

A modification for child support may be initiated by either parent, a caregiver, or by the state.[32] Common reasons a modification may be filed are a change in a parent's income, a change in parenting time, the elimination or addition of expenses considered when child support was originally set, the birth or adoption of a new child to either parent, or the elimination or addition of an extraordinary educational expense or special expense for the child(ren) that are the subject of the case. Where child support was calculated for married couples living separately, modifications are common after divorce because a parenting schedule has been ordered and the payor parent may have more parenting time with the child(ren) than the parenting time days allotted when setting child support.

For a modification to be granted by the court, there must be an upward or downward deviation of at least fifteen percent, which is referred to a significant variance.[33] A significant variance is not required for modifications based on the necessity of providing for the child's health care needs and insurance. Determining whether a significant variance exists is calculated by running a new worksheet and calculator based on the parties' information at the time of the modification hearing and including the current child support obliga-

[32] In case involving Title IV-D services.

[33] The fifteen percent variance requirement is not necessary for parents with monthly income at or below the poverty level.

tion in the appropriate column. The calculator will state if a significant variance exists to modify ongoing child support.

G.
Retroactive Child Support vs. Child Support Arrears

Retroactive child support is defined as a child support obligation retroactively due after the establishment of a child support order and is determined when child support is initially established. For example, the father is ordered to pay child support when his child is three years of age. The court will determine what the father should have paid in child support from the birth of the child to the establishment of the child support obligation, subtract any payments and credits (money paid to the mother or caregiver and certain items purchased for the child) the father is entitled to, and any balance of support that should have been paid but wasn't, is determined and set as retroactive child support. Retroactive child support shall not be awarded for more than five years from the date the action for support is filed unless the court determines for good cause shown,[34] according to Tennessee Code § 36-5-101, that a different award of retroactive child support is in the interest of justice. The burden to show that a longer time period of retroactive support is in the interest of justice is on the person receiving child support. There is a rebuttable presumption that a judgment for retroactive support must be entered by the court when child support is established.[35] The payee parent or custodian may agree to

[34] For child support cases filed after July 1, 2017.

[35] A rebuttable presumption is an assumption made by the court that can be changed upon proof that the court should rule differently.

waive retroactive support and set any obligation at zero. If a retroactive support amount is ordered by the court, a monthly repayment amount towards retroactive support will be added to the ongoing monthly child support obligation.

Child support arrears represent money that the payor parent failed to pay after the child support obligation was ordered by the court. For example, if child support is set at $400 per month against the mother, but the mother misses two months and pays only $200 per month for three months, the mother has now accrued $1,400 in child support arrears.

Interest may accrue on back child support. Collection of retroactive support and arrears may include filing contempt proceedings against the payor, suspension of the payor's driver's license, including commercial licenses; interception of income tax refunds; interception of Social Security back pay; freezing of financial accounts; and interception of settlements and judgments from lawsuits.

Retroactive support obligations and arrears that are not satisfied by the time the ongoing support obligation expires will continue to be due until paid in full and may result in the enforcement of collection efforts even after the child(ren) are grown and living independently.

A payee parent or caregiver may forgive retroactive support and arrears owed to them if certain conditions are met; however, neither the payee parent nor caregiver can forgive any amount owed to the state. Forgiveness of retroactive support, if previously set and ordered by the court, and arrears requires verification that certain conditions have been met along with approval and finalization by the court.

H.
Fast Facts about Child Support

1. Child support received by the payee parent from a third party, for children not the subject of the pending case, is not considered income of the payee parent.
2. A child support obligation may still be due by a parent for a child receiving a monthly derivative from that parent's Social Security or Veterans benefits. Child support will still be owed if the monthly child support obligation is greater than the derivative amount; the payor parent will owe the difference between the monthly child support obligation and the derivative amount received.
3. A derivative benefit greater than the monthly child support that the payor parent would have been ordered to pay does not affect retroactive support or child support arrears. For example, a monthly derivative benefit of $600 and a child support obligation of $400 does not result in $200 being subtracted per month from any retroactive support or arrears obligation.
4. Social Security benefits received by the child due to a disability of the child are not considered when calculating child support.
5. Income earned by minor children is not considered when calculating child support.
6. The income of a parent's spouse is not considered when calculating child support; however, household expenses and lifestyle may be considered.
7. Denial of visitation to the payor parent does not excuse the obligation to pay child support.
8. Stepchildren are not considered when calculating child support.

9. If child support is withheld from the payor's wages, the payor is still reasonable for any amount still due after the withholding (for example, child support is $400 per month, but only $300 is withheld monthly from the payor's wages, the payor must pay the remaining $100 for the month).
10. Once a child support obligation is established, it must be modified by the court; the payor cannot privately pay less (for example, child support is established for two children at $600 per month, the payor cannot decide to only pay $300 or anything less than $600 when the oldest child turns eighteen and graduates high school).
11. The legal obligation to provide health insurance for a child, excluding those children with disabilities, traditionally ends when the child turns eighteen and graduates high school. The law that allows children to remain on their parent's medical insurance into adulthood applies to the insurance providers and permits the parent, if they so elect, to continue to provide coverage but does not make it mandatory for the parent to maintain insurance for an adult child.
12. A child support order alone does not create a visitation order. Often, a payor parent will be allotted days of parenting time when child support is calculated; however, that is not an order for the payor to actually have that amount of parenting time. There must be a visitation order outlining a parenting time schedule for the payor to enforce their visitation.
13. Each parent, and especially the noncustodial parent, should actively maintain a calendar of all parenting time with the child(ren).
14. The payor parent should maintain records and keep all receipts of child support paid directly to the other parent, expenses paid on

behalf of the child(ren), and items purchased for the benefit of the child(ren) to ensure they receive credit when retroactive support is calculated. The payor parent is entitled to a credit only for items purchased that return to the other parent or custodian's home (i.e., the payor parent would not receive a credit for a crib they purchased for their home).

15. A finding of contempt for nonpayment of child support may cause incarceration of the payor parent for a fixed amount of time or until a satisfactory "purge" payment is made. The "purge" payment amount is set by the court and is determined upon the payor's payment and contempt history, the running balance since the last support payment was made, and the financial resources available to the payor. Upon satisfaction of the "purge" payment the payor parent will be released from jail, if no "purge" payment is made the payor parent will serve the jail time ordered by the court for nonpayment of child support.
16. Child support should never be paid in cash to the other parent.
17. Unless a court order states that child support is to be paid directly to the other parent, child support should always be paid through the Tennessee Disbursement Unit. Many Tennessee counties have offices for in-person payments. Payors may also pay via mail, online, and Money Gram.

Chapter 3:
Custody and Visitation (Parenting Time)

To the average person, custody refers to physical possession of the child, but in the law, it extends beyond the physical and is often broken down into two categories: legal custody and physical custody. Legal custody is an extension of parentage; legal custody can be simplified as meaning each parent's parental rights in the eyes of the law. Legal custody may be solely with one parent, primarily with one parent, or joint between the parents. Physical custody is the physical possession of the child and may be solely with one parent, primarily with one parent, or joint between the parents. Visitation is the days and times the parent without primary physical custody exercises parenting time with the child.

This chapter builds upon what we discussed in Chapter 1 and explores custody and visitation once parentage has been established for unmarried persons, and custody and visitation determinations for married couples dissolving their marriage.

Bonus Tidbit: A custodial parent who interferes with the court-ordered parenting time of the other parent may face charges of custodial interference, a criminal offense. A noncustodial parent that exercises physical custody of the child, inconsistent with Tennessee law or court-ordered parenting time may face kidnapping charges, a criminal offense. Civil contempt and criminal contempt may also be brought against a parent for failing to follow a court-ordered parenting schedule.

A.
Primary Residential Parent Designation

Primary residential parent is a legal designation. The primary residential parent, or custodial parent, is the parent with whom the child resides with most of the time and traditionally has primary decision-making power absent a court order. A primary residential parent designation is reserved for unmarried parents and married couples separated or divorced. Where the parents have equal parenting time, the designation of a primary residential parent may be waived or deemed joint by agreement of the parents. Courts may not order parents to waive or share jointly in the primary residential parent designation.

Bonus Tidbit: Unless a Permanent Parenting Plan or court order outlines how major decisions regarding the child(ren) are to be made between the parents, the primary residential parent shall have sole decision making authority.

B.
Joint Legal Custody vs. Joint Physical Custody

Joint legal custody means the parents have the same legal rights towards the child and legal custody is not solely with the mother. Joint physical custody means the parents have equal parenting time with the child.

Married couples automatically have joint legal custody of their children. As discussed in Chapter 2, unmarried mothers have sole legal custody of their children until the father takes legal action through the courts, even if he's already listed on child's birth certificate. Upon an unmarried father establishing his legal paternal rights, the mother's sole legal custody is typically modified to give the parents joint legal custody, with the parent having primary physical custody designed as the primary residential parent.

Married couples also automatically have joint physical custody of their children until the parties separate or divorce. For unmarried couples, the mother has sole physical custody of the child until a parenting schedule is ordered by a court. When parents are unmarried or separating/divorcing, joint physical custody must be agreed to by the parents or ordered by a court. The factors outlined in section C of this chapter are the factors considered by the court in establishing any custody or visitation order, including joint physical custody.

Often parents will have private agreements regarding parenting time. Private agreements of the parents should always be in writing. A private agreement does not give rise to law enforcement involvement or enforcement by the court.[36] However, it can assist the court in determining parenting time if legal action becomes necessary.

---

[36] The police have the authority to enforce court orders including visitation orders.

C.
Establishing a Parenting Schedule

Parenting time or visitation schedules are established by a Permanent Parenting Plan for divorcing parties. For unmarried parents, parenting time or visitation schedules can be established via a Permanent Parenting Plan or a less complex visitation order. A Permanent Parenting Plan is a document created and revised by the State of Tennessee that includes not only a detailed parenting time schedule but also identifies which parent will claim the child(ren) for taxes, who will be responsible for health insurance and uncovered medical expenses, and how certain decisions regarding the child(ren) will be made. Permanent Parenting Plans are required in all divorces with minor children and can either be by agreement of the parents or by order of the court. Permanent Parenting Plans also include the "parental bill of rights" statute,[37] and the parental relocation statute. Less complex visitation orders contain the visitation schedule for the parent receiving visitation, the "parental bill of rights," and other special provisions agreed to by the parents or ordered by the court.

For court-ordered parenting time schedules involving both married and unmarried parents, the court is tasked with establishing a schedule for both parents that will allow each parent to have the maximum participation in the child's life. "Maximum participation" is not a fixed number such as a 50/50 parenting time split between

---

[37] Tennessee Code § 36-6-101 (a)(3)(B)(i) -(ix) (2021).

parents but is rather determined by conducting a "fifteen factor best interest of the child" analysis. The fifteen factors the court considers as outlined in Tennessee Code § 36-6-106 are:

- The strength, nature, and stability of the child's relationship with each parent, including whether one parent has performed most parenting responsibilities relating to the daily needs of the child;
- Each parent's or caregiver's past and potential for future performance of parenting responsibilities, including the willingness and ability of each of the parents and caregivers to facilitate and encourage a close and continuing parent-child relationship between the child and both of the child's parents, consistent with the best interest of the child. In determining the willingness of each of the parents and caregivers to facilitate and encourage a close and continuing parent-child relationship between the child and both of the child's parents, the court shall consider the likelihood of each parent and caregiver to honor and facilitate court-ordered parenting arrangements and rights, and the court shall further consider any history of either parent or any caregiver denying parenting time to either parent in violation of a court order;
- Refusal to attend a court-ordered parent education seminar may be considered by the court as a lack of good faith effort in these proceedings;
- The disposition of each parent to provide the child with food, clothing, medical care, education, and other necessary care;
- The degree to which a parent has been the primary caregiver, defined as the parent who has taken the greater responsibility for performing parental responsibilities;
- The love, affection, and emotional ties existing between each parent and the child;
- The emotional needs and developmental level of the child;

- The moral, physical, mental, and emotional fitness of each parent as it relates to their ability to parent the child. The court may order an examination of a party under Rule 35 of the Tennessee Rules of Civil Procedure and, if necessary for the conducting of the proceedings, order the disclosure of confidential mental health information of a party under § 33-3-105(3). The court order required by § 33-3-105(3) must contain a qualified protective order that limits the dissemination of confidential, protected mental health information to the purpose of the litigation pending before the court and provides for the return or destruction of the confidential, protected mental health information at the conclusion of the proceedings;
  - The child's interaction and interrelationships with siblings, other relatives and step-relatives, and mentors, as well as the child's involvement with the child's physical surroundings, school, or other significant activities;
  - The importance of continuity in the child's life and the length of time the child has lived in a stable, satisfactory environment;
  - Evidence of physical or emotional abuse to the child, to the other parent, or to any other person. The court shall, where appropriate, refer any issues of abuse to Juvenile court for further proceedings;
  - The character and behavior of any other person who resides in or frequents the home of a parent and such person's interactions with the child;
- The reasonable preference of the child if twelve years of age or older. The court may hear the preference of a younger child upon request. The preference of older children should normally be given greater weight than those of younger children;

- Each parent's employment schedule and the court may make accommodations consistent with those schedules; and
- Any other factors deemed relevant by the court.

In cases with custody or visitation disputes, each parent should submit a proposed parenting time schedule to the court.[38] While there is no statutory "minimum" or "standard" parenting time schedule, many Tennessee courts will not award a noncustodial parent less than eighty annual days of visitation without just cause that the noncustodial parent should receive less parenting time.

Bonus Tidbit: While the preference of a child twelve years of age or older is considered, the preference must be consistent with the other statutory factors. Courts have ruled against the child's preference if it's contrary to the child's best interest.

Bonus Tidbit: Upon entry of court-ordered parenting time, a child cannot decide whether they want to visit with the noncustodial parent and the primary residential parent must ensure the other parent is permitted to exercise their court-ordered parenting time.

---

[38] In contested divorce cases, each parent must submit a proposed Permanent Parenting Plan to the court prior to the divorce trial.

D.
Restricting Parenting Time

While parenting time schedules should afford parents maximum participation in their child's life, parenting time restrictions may be ordered by the court if it determines that a parent has engaged in certain conduct. Tennessee law permits restricting parenting time if a parent has willfully abandoned the child for an extended period, has substantially refused to perform parenting responsibilities, or has engaged in the physical abuse, sexual abuse, or a pattern of emotional abuse of the parent, child, or another person living with that child.[39] Parenting time may also be restricted if the parent lives with someone who has engaged in certain physical, sexual, or emotional abuse. There are other reasons for restricting parenting time that require a hearing by the court, including certain impairments of a parent that affect their ability to perform parenting responsibilities and the absence or substantial impairment of emotional ties between the parent and the child.

For an extensive list of factors that a court could consider when determining if a parent's parenting time should be restricted, please see Tennessee Code § 36-6-406.

Courts may order Rule 35 evaluations, paternal evaluations, drug or alcohol screenings, and/or appoint a Guardian Ad Litem in custody

---

[39] Tennessee Code § 36-6-406 (2021).

and visitation disputes if there are credible allegations regarding the mental or physical health of a parent and that parent's ability to care for the child or there are allegations that the child may be exposed to some form of harm while in a parent's care.[40]

[40] A physical or mental evaluation ordered to be conducted on a person if that person's mental or physical health is in controversy. The requirements to obtain a Rule 35 evaluation are listed in Rule 35.01 of the Tennessee Rules of Civil Procedure.; A Guardian Ad Litem is an attorney appointed by the court to represent the interest of the child(ren).

E.
Modification of Parenting Schedule

Once a parenting time schedule is entered with the court, the schedule may only be modified by agreement of the parties or a determination by the court that a material change in circumstances exists to modify the parenting schedule. According to Tennessee law a material change in circumstances does not require a substantial risk of harm to the child but does require a change in circumstances to have occurred since entry of the parenting time schedule with the court.[41] The most common material changes in circumstances are a parent's failure to adhere to the existing parenting time schedule and significant changes in the needs of the child(ren). Tennessee courts have modified custody and awarded primary custody to the other parent where the court has found that the primary residential parent has blatantly and/or repeatedly disregarded the parenting schedule to the detriment of the other parent.

There is no all-encompassing list of circumstances that creates a substantial material change in circumstances, so the particular facts of each case are used to determine if the party seeking the modification has proven a substantial material change in circumstances. In recent

[41] Tennessee Code § 36-6-101 (2021).

years, courts have lowered the threshold for establishing a material change in circumstances.

A modification in custody (changing which parent is designated as the primary residential parent) has a higher burden and requires a finding by the court that the change in circumstances is materially affecting the child's well-being.

Here's a hypothetical situation that demonstrates the difference in seeking a modification of the parenting schedule versus a modification in custody:

Bill and Betty have a custody and visitation order entered by the court designating Betty as the primary residential parent of the parties' seven-year-old daughter and awarding Bill visitation of one weekend per month due to his work schedule. Following entry of the order, Bill obtains a new job with a more flexible schedule. Bill may seek more parenting time with the child based on his more flexible work schedule, and the court is likely to modify the plan to afford Bill greater visitation; however, the change in Bill's work schedule alone will not be enough to support a modification in custody to award Bill primary custody of the parties' daughter.

Bonus Tidbit: When custody needs to be modified due to the death of the primary residential parent, the noncustodial parent needs to file a petition to modify the existing custody order to be properly established as the custodial parent of the child. If no custody order exists, the noncustodial parent must file a petition for custody with the court to obtain legal custody of the child. The noncustodial parent's request for primary custody may be challenged by a third party through a petition for dependency and neglect.

F.
Parental Relocation

The law governing the relocation of a minor child applies only to cases in which a Permanent Parenting Plan or a custody order has been entered with the court. To trigger the relocation statute,[42] the relocating parent must be seeking to relocate the child outside of the state or over fifty miles within the state.[43]

Tennessee law requires a parent who desires to relocate with a minor child to provide notice of their intent to relocate to the other parent. The notice must contain the following:[44]

- Statement of intent to move
- Location of proposed new residence
- Reasons for proposed relocation
- Statement that absent agreement between the parents or an objection by the non-relocating parent within thirty days of the date the notice is sent by registered or certified mail in accordance with applicable statute, the relocating parent may do so by law

---

[42] Tennessee Code § 36-6-108 (2021).

[43] Most parents do not seek to invoke the statute or involve the courts if the parent moves to a neighboring city in another state; for example, father moves with child from Memphis, Tennessee to Olive Branch, Mississippi, which is less than fifty miles away and simply a matter of crossing state lines.

[44] This applies to the primary residential parent. If the noncustodial parent wishes to relocate with the child(ren), they must first file for primary custody of the child(ren).

The fourth notice requirement is confusing, as parents often interpret it to mean they may automatically relocate the child if no objection is made by the non-relocating parent. In reality, if there's no agreement on relocation and a new visitation schedule, the relocating parent must obtain permission to relocate the child from the court. Tennessee Code § 36-6-108 states "Absent agreement by the parents on a new visitation schedule within thirty days of the notice or upon a timely objection in response to the notice, the relocating parent shall file a petition seeking approval of the relocation. The non-relocating parent has thirty days to file a response in opposition to the petition. In the event no response in opposition is filed within thirty days, the parent proposing to relocate with the child shall be permitted to do so."

If a petition regarding relocation is before the court, the court must perform an analysis to determine if relocation is in the best interest of the child based on these eight factors:[45]

- The nature, quality, extent of involvement, and duration of the child's relationship with the parent proposing to relocate and with the non-relocating parent, siblings, and other significant persons in the child's life;
- The age, developmental stage, needs of the child, and the likely impact the relocation will have on the child's physical, educational, and emotional development, taking into consideration any special needs of the child;
- The feasibility of preserving the relationship between the non-relocating parent and the child through suitable visitation ar-

[45] Tennessee Code § 36-6-108 (2021).

rangements, considering the logistics and financial circumstances of the parties;

- The child's preference, if the child is twelve (12) years of age or older. The court may hear the preference of a younger child upon request. The preference of older children should normally be given greater weight than those of younger children;
- Where there is an established pattern of conduct of the relocating parent, either to promote or thwart the relationship of the child and the non-relocating parent;
- Whether the relocation of the child will enhance the general quality of life for both the relocating parent and the child, including, but not limited to, financial or emotional benefit or educational opportunity;
- The reasons of each parent for seeking or opposing the relocation; and
- Any other factor affecting the best interest of the child, including those enumerated in § 36-6-106(a)

Upon the court finding that the relocation is in the best interest of the minor child, the court will modify the parenting time schedule to address the distance between the parties.

Noncustodial parents seeking to relocate should still file to modify the parenting time schedule to address travel and transportation and ensure that the schedule can continue to be followed due to the new residence. For example, a parenting time schedule that affords the noncustodial parent visitation with the child every weekend is unlikely to work when the parent relocates several states away.

Chapter 4:
Annulment and Legal Separation

In Tennessee, the duration of a marriage is not a ground for annulment. A one-month marriage will have to be dissolved through a divorce unless it qualifies for annulment under one of the grounds listed in this chapter. Annulments are strictly reserved for marriages deemed void or voidable. Annulments result in a marriage legally being deemed as never having occurred. While there are several grounds for annulment, the most common annulment cases I have encountered and represented parties in have been on the ground of bigamy. Bigamy makes a marriage void, and when a marriage is void, it must be dissolved by annulment. When a marriage is dissolved by annulment, marital interest in certain assets is extinguished. A divorcing spouse usually has marital interest in their spouse's retirement and other assets, but that interest terminates if an annulment is required to dissolve the marriage. As a special note, it's extremely important to confirm that your future spouse's previous marriages have been properly dissolved, unless widowed, through a court proceeding before marrying them.

This chapter explores the difference in marriages that must be annulled because they are void or incurably invalid versus marriages that are voidable due to a defect that may be cured. This chapter also addresses what happens to assets and property obtained during a marriage that is annulled and how minor children are handled during an annulment.

Legal separation is an alternative to pursuing divorce and is most often filed for religious purposes or when there is a chance for reconciliation. Legal separation may be the best option for some couples, and as such, it is important to be knowledgeable of the inner workings of legal separation versus divorce. Legal separation should not be selected to postpone the inevitable, divorce. This chapter explores the difference between physical separation and legal separation, the grounds for legal separation, and how marital assets and minor children are addressed during a legal separation.

A. Annulment

I. Grounds for Annulment

An annulment means that a marriage is considered void or voidable in the eyes of the law. Once an annulment is granted, the marriage is legally treated as if it never occurred. A marriage is considered void if the defect cannot be cured, such as bigamy and incest. A marriage is considered voidable if the defect, such as insanity or denial of marital rights, could be cured by certain conduct. For voidable marriages, an annulment or a divorce may be filed, but if one spouse is seeking an annulment and the other spouse is seeking a divorce, a court will determine if the spouse seeking an annulment has proven that the marriage is voidable and the defect has not been cured. If so, the marriage will be annulled. For void marriages, the only dissolution is by annulment.

Due to the severe consequences of a marriage being voided, all marriages do not qualify for annulment. In Tennessee, the grounds for annulment, which must exist at the time of the marriage, are:

- **Insanity** – The spouse must be insane at the time of the marriage and for the duration of the marriage. If a spouse that is insane at the time of marriage regains sanity during the marriage and the parties continue the marriage, the court will not annul the marriage on the ground of insanity;
- **Underage** – In Tennessee, the minimum age to marry with parental consent is seventeen. Both parties must be at least seventeen and there can be no more than a four year age difference between the parties seeking to wed. Parental consent requires the parents, guardians, next of kin, or custodians to accompany the

minor(s) when applying for the marriage license and to sign the appropriate affidavit/application. Permission from a court may substitute for parental consent. A court may also grant permission for a minor under the age of seventeen to obtain a marriage license;

- **Incest** – The spouses must be of immediate relation closer than first cousins;
- **Bigamy** – Either spouse has a living husband or wife at the time of marriage;
- **Duress** – A spouse married only due to coercion;
- **Fraud** – A spouse was defrauded by the other spouse into getting married. The fraud must be essential to the marriage to qualify for annulment;
- **Impotence** – A spouse must be permanently unable to physically participate in sexual intercourse. To qualify for annulment, the impotence must have existed at the time the parties were married. The other spouse cannot voluntarily enter the marriage with the knowledge that their spouse has incurable impotency and then seek an annulment on the grounds of impotence; or
- **Denial of marital rights** – A spouse has refused to live with the other spouse or consummate the marriage. To qualify for annulment, the parties must have never lived together or engaged in sexual intercourse, and the election to not live together or engage in intercourse was not by agreement of the parties.

II.
Assets Acquired in a Marriage That Will Be Annulled

Assets such as real property, vehicles, retirement accounts, and bank accounts are commonly acquired during a marriage and are considered marital property (with certain exceptions discussed later). When a marriage is annulled, the assets individually owned are awarded 100 percent to the title holder. Assets jointly titled or owned are treated like items jointly owned by unmarried persons (i.e., friends, relatives, business partners) and the court will divide the items fairly based on the specific factors of the case.

III.
Children Born During a Marriage That Will Be Annulled

Children born during a marriage that is annulled are still treated as if they were born during a valid marriage, and an annulment alone is not a basis to disestablish parentage. Even when a marriage is annulled, a Permanent Parenting Plan, including the calculation of child support, is entered with the court, by agreement or court order, for any minor children born to the parties.

B.
What is Legal Separation?
(Physical Separation Is Not Legal Separation)

While many people mistakenly believe that living separate and apart means they are legally separated, it is not that simple. A true legal separation requires legal action and a court order. The grounds for a legal separation are the same as those for a divorce,[46] but a legal separation means that the parties are still married and will remain married until divorced.

A legal separation is initiated by the filing of a complaint for legal separation. Finalization of a legal separation requires that the parties either enter into a Legal Separation Agreement, outlining division of the marital estate and addressing other provisions such as spousal support and ownership of post-separation assets, or a trial by the court to determine division of the marital estate and awarding of any specific relief sought by the parties. If minor children are involved, a Permanent Parenting Plan is also required in a legal separation action.

Bonus Tidbit: A spouse dating someone after physical separation is often not a concern to the divorce court; however, misspending of marital assets and purchasing of assets for the person the spouse is dating is fair game to be addressed during division of the marital estate. Married persons should never become engaged to third parties, even if physically separated, until they are divorced.

---

[46] Tennessee Code §§ 36-4-101 (2021) and 36-4-102 (2021).; see Chapter 6.

I.
Legal Separation vs. Divorce

Divorce trumps legal separation. If one spouse files for legal separation and the other spouse files for divorce, the court will ultimately grant a divorce unless there is a chance, as acknowledged by both parties, of reconciliation. All the issues, including division of marital assets, parenting time and child support, which would be addressed in a divorce, are addressed in a legal separation. Most parties elect to file for a divorce instead of legal separation; however, there are certain reasons a legal separation may be agreed to by the parties.

II.
Why Legal Separation May Be the Right Choice for a Couple

Legal separation may be the right choice for couples who believe reconciliation is possible, for religious reasons or when certain benefits, such as health insurance and military benefits, may continue via a legal separation but would terminate upon a divorce.

III.
Assets Acquired During Periods of Physical Separation

Property acquired during physical separation is considered marital property unless the property can be classified as separate property under Tennessee law,[47] and the other spouse may be awarded a share of property acquired after physical separation even if they did not contribute to its acquisition. This is most common in pensions, 401(k) accounts, bank accounts, and real property. If the property is in dispute, the court cannot classify it as separate property simply because the parties were separated when it was acquired. Division of property acquired during periods of physical separation will be based on the same twelve factors considered when dividing marital property accumulated before any period of physical separation.[48]

To illustrate how assets acquired during physical separation are subject to division as part of the marital estate, here are a few hypotheticals:

Kyle and Kim decided to separate and live apart ten years ago. Kim has a 401(k) with her employer. The parties have been physically separated for ten years but never filed for a legal separation or divorce. Over the last ten years, Kim's 401(k) has increased by $50,000. Is the $50,000 increase considered marital property? Yes.

---

[47] See Chapter6.
[48] See Chapter 6.

Tina and Tim, married for twenty years, physically separated in 2015. After the physical separation, Tim purchases a new home; Tina is not listed on the mortgage or deed of Tim's home. The property being solely in Tim's name nor the parties being separated means that the house is Tim's separate property. Tim's new house is marital, unless a separate property exception applies as discussed in Chapter 6.

IV.
Assets Acquired After Legal Separation

When marital property is divided under a legal separation agreement or court order, any asset acquired by a spouse after the legal separation is considered the separate property of the spouse who acquired it. If the division of marital property is not addressed via a legal separation agreement, court order, or is reserved,[49] then assets acquired after legal separation will be considered marital unless a separate property exception applies. Therefore, if parties are legally separated but there is no division of the marital assets or articulation of how property acquired during legal separation shall be treated, then its division would have to be addressed upon finalization of a divorce, just like property acquired before the period of legal separation.

[49] The legal separation agreement or court order states that division of the marital estate will be reserved until finalization of a divorce.

Chapter 5:
Uncontested Divorce

Divorce lawyers and courts divide divorces into two categories: uncontested and contested. Most parties hope for an uncontested divorce, but it honestly requires more than one spouse's hope. A divorce may be filed as uncontested or become uncontested during the divorce proceedings due to one spouse not participating in the divorce or the spouses reaching a settlement agreement. For most lawyers, we consider a divorce uncontested at the time of filing only if there is a signed settlement agreement between the parties. If you are interested in pursuing an uncontested divorce and know the whereabouts of your spouse, you will need to discuss settlement terms with your spouse and reach an agreement regarding real property,[50] personal property (financial accounts, retirement accounts, investments, vehicles, furniture, et cetera), debts, spousal support, custody/visitation, and child support to present to your attorney to file an uncontested divorce.

This chapter breaks down what an uncontested divorce is, the different types of uncontested divorces, and what is required for an uncontested divorce.

---

[50] Real property is the legal term for real estate.

A.
What is an Uncontested Divorce?

An uncontested divorce is a divorce in which there are no issues in dispute. A divorce is uncontested either because there is a settlement agreement between the parties, or a default judgment has been entered by the court against one party due to their failure to participate in the divorce proceedings. A divorce may be uncontested at the commencement of the divorce proceedings or become uncontested during the divorce process. For parties to obtain an uncontested divorce by agreement, the agreement requires much more than just an agreement to divorce. Most couples can agree to the divorce and that they should be divorced but can't agree to division of the marital estate, parenting time for the children, and/or financial support. As discussed throughout this chapter, an uncontested divorce by agreement of the parties will always require a Marital Dissolution Agreement, and if minor children are involved, an agreed Permanent Parenting Plan. An uncontested divorce by default judgment requires service on the defendant, and service may be accomplished by personal service or service by publication. An uncontested divorce by default judgment does not include a Marital Dissolution Agreement but will require a court-ordered Permanent Parenting Plan if minor children are involved.

An uncontested divorce is often the most cost-effective and swift divorce option. Divorces without children in Tennessee must be on file with the court for at least sixty days before they are finalized. Divorces with minor children in Tennessee must be on file with the court for least ninety days before they are finalized. Uncontested divorces are usually finalized within ninety to 120 days, including the waiting periods. Contested divorces may take years to finalize, depending on the issues in dispute.

Bonus Tidbit: In all divorces, parties must wait at least thirty days after the finalization of divorce to remarry or acquire additional real property.

B.
Uncontested Divorce by Agreement of the Parties

A divorce may be uncontested by agreement of the parties at the commencement of the divorce filing or become uncontested during the divorce proceedings by a subsequent agreement. For this discussion, we will focus on divorces filed as uncontested because there is an agreement between the parties. As discussed, the agreement must be memorialized in a Marital Dissolution Agreement, and if the parties have minor children, an agreed Permanent Parenting Plan. All divorces begin with the filing a divorce complaint. For uncontested divorces by agreement of the parties, the only divorce ground required to be listed in the divorce complaint is irreconcilable differences. A divorce on the ground of irreconcilable differences is considered a no-fault divorce. Divorce fault grounds are required for contested divorces. Tennessee's divorce grounds are listed in Chapter 6.

If parties desire to have an uncontested divorce but fault must be alleged for religious purposes, then the court will approve the agreed documents offered by the parties but may require testimonial proof regarding the alleged fault. Here, the fault ground(s) must be contained in the divorce complaint.

After filing the divorce complaint, the Marital Dissolution Agreement, and agreed Permanent Parenting Plan, if applicable, the parties must wait the discussed sixty-day or ninety-day waiting period before requesting a hearing to finalize the divorce. The hearing is conducted through the court's uncontested divorce docket. Most courts designate a day each week to hear uncontested divorces and hear multiple uncontested divorces on that day. The uncontested divorce hearing is brief and the plaintiff answers questions asked by their attorney and potentially the court.[51] The court reviews and approves the agreed documents (the Marital Dissolution Agreement and agreed Permanent Parenting Plan), the court enters a Final Decree of Divorce, and declares the parties divorced.[52]

If at the time of filing the divorce complaint, there is no executed Marital Dissolution Agreement and agreed Permanent Parenting Plan, then the divorce must be filed as contested even if there is an oral agreement between the parties. Unfortunately, it is not uncommon for a spouse to say they will agree to certain settlement terms and sign the Marital Dissolution Agreement and agreed Permanent Parenting Plan but then become unresponsive or decline to execute the documents.

---

[51] If the plaintiff is unrepresented, the court will ask the questions.

[52] The court does have the authority to make changes to the terms of the Marital Dissolution Agreement and Permanent Parenting Plan based upon statements of the parties or the documents failing to adequately address certain issues.

C.
Uncontested Divorce by Default Judgment

An uncontested divorce by default judgment begins as a contested divorce and becomes uncontested through certain actions of the parties and orders of the court. A contested divorce cannot be filed on the ground of irreconcilable differences only, and a fault ground or the lack of cohabitation for two or more years with no minor children must be alleged in the complaint for divorce. Divorce complaints filed in contested divorces must be served on the defendant. If the defendant's whereabouts are known, the defendant must be personally served. If the defendant is avoiding personal service or their whereabouts are unknown, then the divorce complaint may be served by publication, which means notice of the divorce proceeding is published in the newspaper designated by the court for service via publication.[53] Upon completion of service, the defendant has thirty days to file an answer to the divorce complaint.[54] If the defendant fails to file an answer, the plaintiff may file for a default judgment against the defendant. A default judgment against the defendant allows the plaintiff to proceed with the divorce without the defendant's participation, and the court will grant a divorce to the plaintiff.

While a default judgment will allow a plaintiff to be granted a divorce without the defendant's involvement in the divorce proceed-

[53] In Shelby County, Tennessee, the newspaper for publication is the *Daily News*.
[54] Additional time is given if service is completed via publication.

ings, the type of divorce relief granted to the plaintiff will depend on how the defendant was served. Once the default judgment is granted, the plaintiff must wait at least thirty days before setting the divorce for a final hearing. The divorce is set for hearing on the uncontested divorce docket. Uncontested divorces granted via a default judgment require a witness to testify on behalf of the plaintiff.

Bonus Tidbit: A default judgment and subsequent uncontested divorce by default may be set aside and reopened if the defendant can prove a valid and legal reason exists to set aside the default judgment and allow the defendant to participate in the divorce and address requested relief regarding financial support, the marital estate, and minor children, if applicable.[55]

---

[55] Tennessee Rules of Civil Procedure, Rule 60.02.

I.
Personal Service of Defendant

A defendant may be personally served via a private process server, a member of the sheriff's department, or certified mail. Once a defendant is personally served, they have thirty days to formally file an answer to the complaint for divorce. If no answer is filed, then the motion for default judgment may be filed by the plaintiff and the court will grant a default judgment against the defendant. Following entry of the order granting a default judgment against the defendant, the plaintiff must wait at least thirty days before setting the hearing on the court's uncontested divorce docket. While the divorce is heard and finalized through the court's uncontested divorce docket, the plaintiff must complete additional steps since the divorce is uncontested by way of default judgment. At the uncontested divorce hearing, the plaintiff must present a witness that can testify with personal knowledge regarding the grounds for divorce alleged against the defendant. If the plaintiff is seeking any specific relief regarding spousal support, division of marital assets, allocation or marital debt, or attorney fees, the plaintiff is still required to offer proof to support the relief sought. If minor children are involved, the plaintiff must present a proposed Permanent Parenting Plan outlining their suggested parenting schedule and child support calculations. Courts are not required to order the relief sought by the plaintiff or approve the plaintiff's proposed Permanent Parenting Plan; even though the defendant is not present to object, the court will still conduct the appropriate analysis for the requested relief. Therefore, uncontested divorces via default judgment are not a "free-for-all" in which the plaintiff gets to present a wish list; the plaintiff must prove why they are entitled to the relief they are seeking.

II.
Service via Publication

If a plaintiff cannot locate the defendant after reasonable efforts, the plaintiff may request that service be issued via publication, which is a legal process of publishing the divorce filing notice in the court-designated newspaper. Reasonable efforts include contacting family and friends of the defendant, attempting to serve the defendant at their last known address or place of employment, calling and emailing the defendant, and attempting to locate or contact the defendant via social media. Tennessee law outlines how long the notice must run in the newspaper and the contents of the notice.[56] For divorces, notice must be published for a minimum of four weeks. If the defendant's last known residence is outside of the state or the county in which the divorce was filed, it is proper to publish service in the appropriate newspaper in the defendant's last known county.

A divorce requiring service via publication is considered a contested divorce, and a default judgment is necessary. If the defendant does not answer the complaint for divorce after the publication has expired,[57] then the plaintiff may pursue a default judgment.

Upon completion of service via publication, filing of the motion for default judgment, entry of the default judgment, and the order

---

[56] Tennessee Code § 21-1-204 (2021).

[57] The published notice will list a date and time for the defendant to answer the divorce complaint.

granting default judgment being filed for at least thirty days, the divorce will also be set on the court's uncontested divorce docket. Just like uncontested divorces in which the defendant was personally served, the plaintiff must present a witness who can testify with personal knowledge regarding the grounds for divorce alleged against the defendant.

A court may decline to address the division of marital assets, awards of spousal support, allocation of marital debt, or issues concerning minor children in a divorce in which service was completed by publication. Service via publication will allow a divorce to be granted without the participation of both parties, but certain issues are often reserved until the defendant's whereabouts are ascertained and the defendant may be personally served. The court does this because there is a question of if the defendant actually received notice of the divorce proceedings when service was completed through publication, opposed to the court knowing that a defendant that was personally served received notice.

Bonus Tidbit: Witnesses for uncontested divorces, via default judgment, should be at least 18 years of age and have personal knowledge of plaintiff's ground(s) for divorce. For example, if the ground for divorce was lack of cohabitation for at least two or more years with no minor children, then a witness who has only known the plaintiff for a few months lacks personal knowledge that the parties have been separated for at least two years.

D.
Uncontested Divorce Documents: Marital Dissolution Agreement and Agreed Permanent Parenting Plan

A Marital Dissolution Agreement is a written voluntary contract between divorcing spouses outlining their divorce settlement agreement. The Marital Dissolution Agreement will contain provisions regarding alimony, division of real property, division of personal property, division of retirement accounts, health insurance coverage, life insurance policies, division of any businesses, and allocations of debt. Often divorcing parties will say, "We don't have anything," or "We don't want anything from each other." A Marital Dissolution Agreement is required in all uncontested divorces and reflects whatever the settlement agreement is even if the parties don't have significant assets or are not seeking anything from the other party.

Here are a few examples of provisions in Marital Dissolution Agreements addressing alimony, real property, and allocation of debts.

a. Parties agree to wife receiving alimony:

"Wife shall be awarded transitional alimony in the monthly amount of $1,000 per month for twenty-four months commencing on the 1st day of the month following entry of the Final Decree of Divorce in this matter. Husband shall remit payment to wife in equal installments of $500.00 on the 1st and 15th day of each month. Payment shall be remitted via electronic funds transfer (i.e., CashApp, Venmo, PayPal, or bank wire). Wife shall be permitted to pursue issuance of a wage assignment order against husband if he misses a payment and fails to become current within thirty days of that missed payment or if husband becomes consecutively late on more than two (2) payments in a six (6) month period. Payments are considered late after the 5th and 20th day of each month."

b. Parties agree that neither party shall receive alimony:

"Husband and wife waive any separate and distinct claim to any alimony, now and in the future."

c. Wife owns premarital real property:

"The parties do not jointly own any real property. Wife owns real property located at 1234 Main Avenue, Middle, Tennessee 11111 which was acquired prior to the date of marriage. Wife is vested all rights, title and interest in the aforementioned property and husband is divested of the same. Husband shall vacate the residence within thirty days of executing this Marital Dissolution Agreement. Wife shall be solely responsible for all financial obligations associated with the aforementioned real property, including but not limited to the mortgage, homeowner's insurance, property taxes, maintenance, and repairs."

d. Parties do not own any real property:

The parties do not own any real property, jointly or separately."

e. Parties do not have any debt in both spouses' names and each spouse is to pay their individual debts:

"Each party shall be solely responsible for all debts held in their individual name. Subject to the provisions of this Marital Dissolution Agreement, wife shall not at any time after execution of this Marital Dissolution Agreement incur any debt or obligation for which husband or his estate may be or become liable. If wife does incur such a debt, wife shall indemnify and hold harmless husband to the full extent of the amount of the debt, including interest, expenses, legal expenses and attorney fees. Subject to the provisions of the Marital

Dissolution Agreement, husband shall not at any time after execution of this Marital Dissolution Agreement incur any debt or obligation for which wife or her estate may be or become liable. If husband does incur such a debt, husband shall indemnify and hold harmless wife to the full extent of the amount of the debt, including interest, expenses, legal expenses and attorney fees."

Besides the Marital Dissolution Agreement outlining the settlement terms of the parties, it also includes mandatory provisions regarding the parties' voluntary consent to the agreement, full disclosure of assets, the parties' acknowledgment they believe the agreement is both fair and equitable, waiver of service and the Servicemembers Civil Relief Act, consent to the court's jurisdiction, and that the parties have received certain notices regarding health insurance and creditors' ability to collect debts. The Marital Dissolution Agreement also addresses attorney fees, court costs, surname changes, and contains other mandatory language.

The Marital Dissolution Agreement is signed by both parties in the presence of a notary public and filed with the court. Once a Marital Dissolution Agreement is filed with the court, a spouse may only withdraw their consent or request that the court reject the agreement in very limited circumstances; therefore, it is very important for both parties to be fully aware of what they are agreeing to before signing a Marital Dissolution Agreement. Uncontested divorces must be finalized within six months of the execution date of the Marital Dissolution Agreement. If the divorce is not finalized within six months, the parties must sign an updated Marital Dissolution Agreement or an addendum to the existing agreement reaffirming their consent. Intentionally delaying the finalization of the divorce to get out of the Marital Dissolution Agreement is not encouraged and could cause great consequences from the court.

An agreed Permanent Parenting Plan as an agreement between divorcing spouses that addresses all issues regarding the parties' minor children. In Tennessee, Permanent Parenting Plans are drafted and revised by the state, so it is important to ensure parties are using the most current version of the form when entering into a Permanent Parenting Plan. An agreed Permanent Parenting Plan will designate a primary residential parent, or state that the parties waive the designation or will share jointly in the designation. An agreed Permanent Parenting Plan outlines the day-to-day, holiday, and school break parenting time schedule the parties have agreed to. An agreed Permanent Parenting Plan will also contain the agreement reached by the parties regarding claiming the child(ren) on tax returns, providing health insurance coverage for the children, and major decision making for the children. Permanent Parenting Plans also include child support calculations, and a child support worksheet must be attached to the plan unless child support has been established by another court. If so, that court's order must be attached to the plan. Permanent Parenting Plans also include mandatory provisions such as the "paternal bill of rights," the paternal relocation statute and notice, transportation and exchanging of the child(ren), and other language required by the state.

Bonus Tidbit: In any divorce in which the wife is pregnant by the husband, birth of the child is required before the divorce is finalized as parenting time and child support cannot be addressed and established until the child's birth.

Bonus Tidbit: In Tennessee, all divorcing parents with minor children must complete a parent education seminar and present their certificate of completion to the court. The seminar is a four-hour course with online options available. The parents do not have to complete the seminar together.

Chapter 6:
Contested Divorce

Contested divorces are not exclusive to the wealthy, high profile, or narcissistic. A divorce may be contested for several reasons, including the whereabouts of one spouse being unknown (as discussed in Chapter 5), the parties being unable to agree on what happens to an asset, both parties wanting primary custody of the minor children, or one spouse not wanting the divorce. This chapter highlights what a contested divorce is, what makes up the marital estate, the factors a court considers when dividing marital assets, how custody and visitation are addressed, and other common issues in contested divorces.

A.
What is a Contested Divorce?

A contested divorce is simply defined as a divorce in which there is no agreement regarding the marital estate or parenting time and child support regarding shared minor children. The most common contested divorces are divorces in which both parties desire to be divorced but cannot agree on how certain marital assets are to be divided, if spousal support is feasible, how much parenting time each parent should have with the minor children, the value of marital assets, who should pay which debts, et cetera.

A contested divorce is initiated by filing a complaint for divorce. The complaint must contain certain things, including the statistical information of the parties, the identification of any marital real property, certain information regarding minor children, the alleged ground(s) for divorce, and the specific relief (i.e., spousal support, designation as primary residential parent, awarding of real property, et cetera) sought by the plaintiff. A contested divorce cannot properly be filed on the exclusive ground of irreconcilable differences. While irreconcilable differences should be listed as a ground, one of the following grounds must be alleged in the contested complaint for divorce as outlined by Tennessee statute:[58]

- Either party, at the date of the marriage, was and still is naturally impotent and incapable of procreation;

[58] Tennessee Code § 36-4-101 (2021).

- Either party has knowingly entered into a second marriage, in violation of a previous marriage still subsisting;[59]
- Either party has committed adultery;
- Willful or malicious desertion or absence of either party, without a reasonable cause for one whole year;
- Being convicted of any crime that, by the laws of the state, renders the party infamous;
- Being convicted of a crime that, by the laws of the state, is declared to be a felony, and sentenced to confinement in the penitentiary;
- Either party has attempted to take the life of the other, by poison or any other means showing malice;
- Refusal, by a spouse, to move with their spouse to this state, without a reasonable cause, and being willfully absent from the spouse residing in Tennessee for two years;
- The woman was pregnant at the time of the marriage, by another person, without the knowledge of the husband;
- Habitual drunkenness or abuse of narcotic drugs of either party, when the spouse has contracted either such habit after marriage;
- The husband or wife is guilty of such cruel and inhuman treatment or conduct toward the spouse as renders cohabitation unsafe and improper, which may also be referred to in pleadings as inappropriate marital conduct;

---

[59] The spouse of the second marriage must seek to dissolve the marriage by annulment as the second marriage is void. The spouse of the first marriage would pursue divorce on the ground of bigamy due to the spouse entering a second marriage prior to the legal dissolution of the first marriage. The spouse of the first marriage would not qualify for an annulment on the ground of bigamy as the first marriage is legally valid.

- The husband or wife has offered such indignities to the spouse's person as to render the spouse's position intolerable, and forced the spouse to withdraw;
- The husband or wife has abandoned the spouse or forced the spouse out of the shared residence for no just cause and has refused or neglected to provide for the spouse while having the ability to so provide; or
- For a continuous period of two or more years that commenced before or after April 18, 1985, both parties have lived in separate residences, have not cohabited as man and wife during such period, and there are no minor children of the parties.

There are defenses to the grounds for divorce, more specifically justifiable cause as a defense to inappropriate marital conduct and connivance, condonation, and recrimination as defenses to adultery. To raise the defense of connivance against adultery, the spouse accused of adultery must prove that their spouse knowingly assisted in the adulterous conduct; knowing assistance may include permitting the spouse to promote prostitution, voyeurism, or paying for the spouse to engage in sexual acts with third parties. The defense of condonation is proper if the spouse alleging adultery forgave the cheating spouse after the extramarital relationship or sexual conduct and the spouses resumed marital relations after the known adultery. Recrimination as a defense to adultery means that the alleging spouse is also guilty of committing adultery.

A contested divorce can eventually be converted to an uncontested divorce if the parties reach a settlement before having a divorce trial or via a default judgment, as discussed in Chapter 5.

In a contested divorce, the defendant must file an answer to the divorce complaint. In the defendant's answer, they must admit or deny the information in the plaintiff's divorce complaint. In addition to filing an answer, the defendant should always file a counter-complaint for divorce to ensure the defendant is able to allege fault against the plaintiff, request and receive specific relief,[60] and proceed with the divorce if the plaintiff either dismisses their complaint for divorce or fails to continue participating in the divorce proceedings.

Bonus Tidbit: Upon the filing of a complaint for divorce, annulment, or legal separation, the following mandatory injunctions are issued and notice of these injunctions must be given to both parties. Many courts in Tennessee have a pre-typed form outlining the injunctions to be filed with the divorce, annulment, or legal separation complaint. Lawyers and parties representing themselves should ensure that the mandatory injunctions notice is filed with the court and properly served. Violation of a mandatory injunction may result in a finding of civil contempt, criminal contempt, or other action by the court. The mandatory injunctions notice states as follows:

Pursuant to T.C.A. Section 36-4-106, the following injunctions are issued against each party effective at the filing of this Complaint for Divorce/Legal Separation/Annulment and upon personal service or waiver and acceptance of service of Respondent/Defendant:

- (A) Each party is restrained and enjoined from transferring, assigning, borrowing against, concealing or in any way dissipating or disposing of any marital property without the consent of the other party or an order of the court. (B) Expenditures from current income to maintain the marital standard of living and usual and ordinary costs of operating a business are not restricted by this

---

[60] Specific relief includes spousal support/alimony, allocation of debts, proposed division of the marital estate, and attorney fees.

injunction. Each party shall maintain records of all expenditures, copies of which shall be available to the other party upon request;

- Each party is restrained and enjoined from voluntarily canceling, modifying, terminating, assigning, or allowing to lapse for non-payment of premiums, any insurance policy including, but not limited to life, health, disability, homeowners, renters and automobile, where such insurance policy provides coverage to either of the parties or the children, or that names either of the parties of the children as beneficiaries, without the consent of the other party or an order of the court. "Modifying" includes any change in beneficiary status;
- Each party is restrained from harassing, threatening, assaulting or abusing the other and from making disparaging remarks about the other in the presence of any children of the parties or to either party's employer;
- Each party is restrained and enjoined from hiding, destroying or spoiling, in whole or in part, any evidence electronically stores or on computer hard drives or other memory storage devices;
- Each party is restrained from removing the children of the parties from the State of Tennessee, or more than fifty miles from the marital home, without the permission of the other party or an order of the court, unless in the case of a removal based upon well-founded fear of physical abuse against either the fleeing parent or the child. In such cases, upon request of the non-relocating parent, the court will conduct an expedited hearing, by phone conference, if appropriate, to determine the reasonableness of the relocation and to make such other orders as appropriate;
- The provisions of Section 36-6-101(a)(3) shall be applicable upon fulfillment of the requirements of subsection (d) of this act;

- This injunction shall not preclude either party from applying to the court for further temporary orders, an expanded injunction or modifications or revocation of this temporary injunction; and
- This temporary injunction remains in effect against both parties until the Final Decree of Divorce or Order of Legal Separation is entered, the petition is dismissed, the parties reach agreement or until the Court modifies or dissolves the injunction.

B.
Spouse Unwilling to Agree to Divorce Terms

One spouse may be unwilling to agree to divorce terms for a variety of reasons including not wanting a divorce, being too emotional to think rationally, or sincerely not agreeing with the settlement terms proposed by their spouse.

It is not uncommon for a spouse who did not agree to an uncontested divorce when approached by their spouse, or who procrastinated when presented with settlement documents before filing of the contested complaint for divorce, to agree to an uncontested divorce and sign the settlement documents once they have been served with the contested paperwork. Unfortunately, some spouses will not take the spouse seeking a divorce seriously until they are served and realize that their spouse wants a divorce with or without a settlement.

While a contested divorce is pending in the court, certain temporary relief may be sought and awarded. Temporary relief includes orders of protections, injunctions, temporary spousal support, temporary child support, temporary visitation, being awarding temporary exclusive possession of the marital residence, and interim attorney fees.

Discovery is also completed while a contested divorce is pending. Discovery may include issuing interrogatories (questions issued to a party by the opposing counsel that must be answered in writing, witnessed by a notary public, and submitted to the court and opposing counsel), requesting the production of certain documents, seeking admissions, conducting depositions, evaluating businesses, issuing subpoenas for financial records, and hiring experts.

C.
Most Common Disputes in Contested Divorces
I. Alimony

Alimony often prevents parties from settling because many people are misinformed about alimony. Alimony is not automatically awarded in any divorce. The spouse seeking alimony must make a specific request and be the economically disadvantaged spouse. There are twelve factors that the court considers when determining if alimony should be awarded, the type of alimony that should be awarded, the duration of the alimony payments, and the amount of alimony:[61]

- Each spouse's earning ability, financial resources, financial obligations (bills and debt), and financial needs (do they have a monthly deficit);
- Each spouse's education and professional training, the ability of each spouse to obtain education and professional training, and the need for a spouse to obtain education and/or professional training to reasonably improve their earning ability or increase their income;
- The duration of the marriage;
- The age and mental condition of each party;

[61] Tennessee Code § 36-5-121 (2021).

- The physical condition of each party, including, but not limited to, physical disability or incapacity due to chronic debilitating disease;
- The extent to which it would be undesirable for a party to seek employment outside the home because such party will be the custodian of a minor child of the marriage;
- The separate assets of each party, both real and personal, tangible and intangible;
- How marital property has been divided or awarded between the parties;
- The standard of living of the parties established during the marriage;
- Each spouse's tangible and intangible contributions to the marriage, either financially or as a homemaker, and each spouse's tangible and intangible contributions toward the other spouse's education, training, or earning ability;
- the relative fault of the parties, where the court, in its discretion, deems it appropriate to do so; and
- Such other factors, including the tax consequences to each party, that are necessary to consider the equities between the parties.

While the court considers all these factors, the primary focus is on the financial need of the economically disadvantaged spouse and the ability of the other spouse to offer financial support. Alimony is not awarded simply because a spouse seeks it, nor is it punitive; there must be a sincere need for financial support and an ability to provide spousal support. While alimony is not awarded as punishment for a spouse's wrongdoings, fault is a defense against requests for alimony. Therefore, an abusive or cheating spouse's request for alimony may be denied upon a finding of fault by the court.

The Tennessee Court of Appeals has held that alimony cannot result in a financial deficit for the payor spouse. If the parties have minor children, child support is calculated before the court considers any request for alimony. Except for awards of temporary spousal support while the divorce is pending, the marital estate must be divided before the calculation and awarding of any post-divorce alimony.

Bonus Tidbit: Temporary spousal support may be providing monetary support directly to a spouse or being ordered to pay and maintain certain marital debts, including housing (mortgage or rent), car notes, loans, credit cards, utilities, and cell phones.

There are four types of alimony in Tennessee:[62]

- Rehabilitative alimony – In Tennessee, rehabilitative alimony is the preferred type of alimony award in divorces. Rehabilitative alimony is the monetary support of a financially disadvantaged spouse for a fixed duration of time to allow the disadvantaged spouse to obtain education and training to financially rehabilitate themselves to obtain a post-divorce standard of living reasonably comparable to the standard of living experienced during the marriage or the expected post-divorce standard of living of the other spouse. Rehabilitative alimony will be awarded only if rehabilitation is reasonably feasible. Age, health, existing education, and training are all factors considered when determining if rehabilitation is feasible. Sometimes, rehabilitation may only be partially feasible, and in those cases, the court may award a certain amount in rehabilitative alimony support. Then, upon partial rehabilita-

---

[62] Tennessee Code § 36-5-121 (2021).

tion, a court will award a lesser amount in permanent alimony (legally known as alimony in futuro).

- Alimony in futuro/periodic alimony – Alimony in futuro is long-term spousal support; long-term may be permanent or for an extended period. Alimony in futuro is typically reserved for cases in which a spouse cannot rehabilitate themselves because of age, health, and/or very limited educational ability or training. In addition to rehabilitation not being feasible, alimony in futuro is most common in long-term marriages. Alimony in futuro is sometimes referred to "alimony forever," but that is not true. Even in awards of permanent alimony, alimony in futuro may be modified or terminated upon a substantial and material change in circumstances, such as the spouse receiving alimony remarrying, or the payor spouse experiencing a financial hardship.
- Transitional Alimony – Transitional alimony is alimony awarded to assist a spouse that is not in need of rehabilitation but needs financial assistance to aid in transitioning from the joint income and financial resources of a marriage to maintaining themselves on their sole income and financial resources. Transitional alimony is awarded to combat the economic consequences the disadvantaged spouse may experience as the result of divorce, legal separation, or other proceedings, such as orders of protection. Transitional alimony is generally awarded for a duration of time shorter than any other form of alimony.
- Alimony in solido/lump sum alimony – Alimony in solido is a support award of a fixed and certain amount either paid as a lump sum or via installments to address or balance an imbalance between the spouses resulting from an equal property division. While alimony in solido is not limited to attorney fees, the order-

ing of a spouse to pay the other spouse's attorney fees is often classified as alimony in solido.

Rehabilitative alimony and alimony in futuro are modifiable (increase, decrease, or terminate). Alimony in solido is considered a final judgment and is non-modifiable and does not terminate upon remarriage or death. Transitional alimony is modifiable only if expressly designated as such at the time it was awarded. However, a rebuttable presumption for modification of transitional alimony will exist if the person receiving transitional alimony is living with a third party and certain factors are met. The types of alimony may be awarded separately or in combination except for rehabilitative alimony and transitional alimony, which cannot be awarded together, as transitional alimony is proper only if the disadvantaged spouse does not need rehabilitation.

A complaint for separate maintenance may be filed in lieu of a complaint for divorce or legal separation. A complaint for separate maintenance is most common in cases where an order of protection has been entered against one spouse and the other spouse needs immediate financial support.

Bonus Tidbit: Alimony will not be awarded in a marriage dissolved by annulment.

Bonus Tidbit: A spouse may sue their spouse for monetary damages if torts have been committed against them by their spouse. Torts include assault, battery, and unwilling transmittal of a sexually transmitted disease.

II.
Division of Marital Estate

The marital estate is the combination of marital assets and debts. A simple definition of marital assets is anything acquired during the marriage, with certain exceptions, with a monetary value. Marital assets include but are not limited to income, real property, financial accounts, furniture, appliances, electronics, stocks, bonds, collectibles, businesses, business inventory, business equipment, cars, digital currencies, and retirement accounts. Just because property is titled in one spouse's name does not mean it is separate property, especially if acquired during the marriage. It is often marital property unless the property can be classified as separate property, which is defined in this chapter.

Spouses often have a habit of saying "My money" and "I paid for that," or "They didn't contribute anything." Money earned during the marriage, with a very few exceptions, is marital. It doesn't matter which spouse earned it or if it was deposited into a separate account. The same applies for items purchased with money earned during the marriage (i.e., real property, furniture, vehicles, et cetera).

Before the division of any assets or debts, the court must first determine if the property is separate or marital. Separate property must be awarded to the owner spouse and cannot be divided by the court. A spouse may claim an interest in property that would be classified as separate property if that spouse can prove the transmutation or commingling of the separate property with marital property. The spouse claiming transmutation or commingling must allege that their spouse's separate property is now marital and prove their claim.

Bonus Tidbit: Do not add a spouse's name to your separate property unless you intend for the property to become marital.

Separate property is legally defined as:[63]

- All real and personal property owned by a spouse before marriage, including, but not limited to, assets held in individual retirement accounts (IRAs) as that term is defined in the Internal Revenue Code of 1986 (26 U.S.C.);
- Property acquired in exchange for property acquired before the marriage;
- Income from and appreciation of property owned by a spouse before marriage, unless each party substantially contributed to its preservation and appreciation;
- Property acquired by a spouse at any time by gift or inheritance;
- Pain and suffering awards, a victim of crime compensation awards, future medical expenses, and future lost wages;
- Property acquired by a spouse after an order of legal separation where the court has made a final disposition of property.

Property that cannot be defined as separate is deemed as marital. Marital property is defined as "all real and personal property, both tangible and intangible, acquired by either or both spouses during the course of the marriage up to the date of the final divorce hearing and owned by either or both spouses".[64] Marital property also includes retirement and financial accounts, vested and unvested, that accrued during the marriage due to employment held by either spouse during

[63] Tennessee Code § 36-4-121 (2021).
[64] Tennessee Code § 36-4-121 (2021).

the marriage.[65] Funds held in such accounts before the date of marriage are subtracted out and held as separate property.[66] Funds that accrued after the date of marriage are subject to equitable division as part of the marital estate. Recovery in personal injury, workers' compensation, and Social Security disability claims are also marital property if the money is received for lost wages (during the marriage), damage to marital property, or medical bills paid with marital funds. Once the property has been classified as separate or marital, the court determines how the marital property should be equitably divided in accordance with these statutory factors:

- The duration of the marriage;
- The age, physical and mental health, vocational skills, employability, earning capacity, estate, financial liabilities, and financial needs of each party;
- The tangible or intangible contribution by one party to the education, training or increased earning power of the other party;
- The relative ability of each party for future acquisitions of capital assets and income;
- The contribution of each party to the acquisition, preservation, appreciation, depreciation, or dissipation of the marital or separate property, including the contribution of a party to the marriage as homemaker, wage earner, or parent, with the contribution of a party as homemaker or wage earner to be given the same weight if each party has fulfilled its role. Dissipation means wasteful disposal of marital property for a purpose contrary to the marriage;

---

[65] Retirement accounts include pensions, 401(k)s, Thrift Savings Plans, et cetera.; Financial accounts include investments, banking accounts, stock options, et cetera.
[66] Including appreciation in the funds.

- The value of the separate property of each party;
- The estate of each party at the time of the marriage;
- The economic circumstances of each party at the time the division of property is to become effective;
- The tax consequences to each party, costs associated with the reasonably foreseeable sale of the asset, and other reasonably foreseeable expenses associated with the asset;
- In determining the value of an interest in a closely held business or similar asset, all relevant evidence, including valuation methods typically used regarding such assets without regard to whether the sale of the asset is reasonably foreseeable. Depending on the characteristics of the asset, such considerations could include, but would not be limited to, a lack of marketability discount, a discount for lack of control, and a control premium, if any should be relevant and supported by the evidence;
- The amount of Social Security benefits available to each spouse; and
- Such other factors necessary to consider the equities between the parties.

Fault is not considered when dividing the marital estate. Therefore an alcoholic or cheating spouse does not get less from the marital estate because they committed adultery or are a habitual drinker. Equitable does not mean equal, nor does it mean that each spouse receives a portion of each asset. When there is real property with equity and no other assets, the property may either be sold and the proceeds divided between the parties, or the spouse retaining the property may be ordered to refinance the property to pay the other spouse their share of equity.[67] When minor children or adult children with special needs are involved, the court may give special consideration to the spouse who will have primary custody of the children when awarding the real property.

There is a rebuttal presumption that debts acquired during the marriage are marital, even if the debt is in only one spouse's name. While there are no statutory factors for dividing debts, the court applies the principle of equitable division. The court considers why the debt was incurred, how the debt benefitted the marriage, the division of marital assets, and each spouse's relative ability to repay the debt.[68] Debts may be allocated to one spouse or divided between the parties as the court deems appropriate based upon the facts. In Tennessee, the allocation of debt in a divorce does not affect a creditor's ability to pursue the spouse that signed a contractual agreement regarding the debt[69]. Therefore, a former spouse cannot use the divorce order to not pay a debt if creditors attempt collection. The former spouse would need to return to divorce court and seek reimbursement against their former spouse ordered to pay the debt for any amount the creditor collected from them.[70]

---

[67] In divorces, real property is typically the marital residence but may be other properties and/or land owned by the parties.

[68] Benefits to the marriage may be direct or indirect. A direct benefit would be paying the utility bill for the marital household. An indirect benefit would be a spouse's car note, as a vehicle purchased during the marriage would be marital property.

[69] This notice to the parties applies in uncontested and contested divorce and is always contained in the parties' Marital Dissolution Agreement and Final Decree of Divorce.

[70] This applies to monies collected by the creditor after the other party was ordered to be responsible for the debt.

Bonus Tidbit: It is extremely important to know the bank accounts of your spouse, their income, revenue generated from any business (separate or marital) your spouse has an interest in, assets owned by your spouse (i.e. stocks, bonds, digital currency, collectibles, and investment accounts), retirement accounts owned by your spouse, marital debt, and any separate debt of your spouse. This information is always necessary in a contested divorce.

III.
Custody and Parenting Time

Children born to married parents are legitimated at birth and the spouses share joint legal custody of the children. At the time of finalizing a divorce, legal separation, or annulment, parenting time must be addressed, and a Permanent Parenting Plan must be entered with the court.

As discussed in Chapter 2, child support may be requested and awarded in cases where a married couple is living apart, and there is no requirement that the parties' have filed for divorce, legal separation, or an annulment. In these cases, a child support order is not an order establishing primary custody for one of the spouses, but rather is simply awarded to the spouse with whom the child(ren) has resided most of the time with during the parents' period of physical separation. An award of temporary child support during the pendency of a divorce, legal separation, or annulment is also not an order of primary custody to either parent.

For married couples, custody and visitation may be addressed only by a court via a divorce, legal separation, or annulment. The only exception to this is the filing of dependency and neglect by one parent against the other parent.

While a divorce, legal separation, or annulment is pending, either parent may request temporary parenting time from the court by filing a petition and presenting a proposed temporary Parenting Plan.

Absent an emergency or an active order of protection, parties must attend mediation before the court will address temporary parenting time.[71] The parent asking the court to address temporary parenting time must file a proposed temporary Parenting Plan and if the other parent fails to file a competing proposed temporary Parenting Plan, the court may approve and enter the requesting parent's proposed temporary plan. In a contested divorce, both parties must present a proposed Permanent Parenting Plan and must offer proof at trial as to why the court should approve their proposed plan. The court has the discretion to adopt one parent's proposed plan or draft its own parenting plan.

The same factors outlined in Chapter 3 are considered when determining a parenting schedule in a divorce case and the parenting schedule must balance maximum participation for the parents with the best interest of the child(ren). The appropriate parenting schedule is unique to the facts of a case; Tennessee higher courts have reversed courts' parenting schedules if there is a finding that the parenting schedule ordered did not afford each parent maximum participation based upon the particular facts of the case.

Once a Permanent Parenting Plan is entered with the court, it may only be modified by agreement of the parents, or by the court if it determines there is a material change in circumstances. Once a Permanent Parenting Plan is entered, custody or parenting time will not be temporarily modified absent the court determining there is an immediate threat of irreparable harm to the child unless immediate action is taken.

---

[71] Mediation is also required, absent an order of protection or waiver by the court, in all contested divorces with children.

Bonus Tidbit: I'm often asked if a divorced parent may leave custody of minor children to a third party if they die before the children becoming adults. The answer is no. Custody would pass to the other parent unless it is shown to the court that the other parent is unfit or that it is not in the children's best interest for the other parent to assume primary custody.

Bonus Tidbit: In extraordinary cases, stepparents may be awarded responsible visitation with their stepchildren as part of a divorce or legal separation if certain factors exist and the court determines visitation is in the best interest of the child.[72] The ordering of stepparent visitation invokes no paternal rights towards the child nor does it trigger entry of a Permanent Parenting Plan.

---

[72] Tennessee Code § 36-6-303 (2021).

Chapter 7:
Adoptions

An adoption is the legal process of permanently transferring the parental rights and responsibilities of a child from the biological parent(s) to the adoptive parent(s). Upon finalization of an adoption, the adoptive parent(s) and child shall have the same legal relationship as a child with their natural parents. The legal relationship created by an adoption may not always be the same relationship recognized by the adoptive parent(s) and child. For example, often in grandparent adoptions, the child and grandparent's relationship remains the same in their day-to-day life, while legally the grandparent is the mother or father of their grandchild.

Adoptions may be open, closed, private, and/or state-sponsored. Private adoptions are adoptions in which there is no state involvement. Common private adoptions are stepparent adoptions and adoptions through adoption agencies. State-sponsored adoptions are those in which the State of Tennessee is involved because the child is in the custody of the state (i.e., foster care) or in the foster care system of another state. Closed adoptions are those in which the record(s) and identifying information are sealed and communication between the biological parent(s) and the adopted child is prohibited. With open adoptions, the biological parents participate in the adoption placement process and may maintain a relationship with the child post-adoption. This chapter discusses the different types of adoptions, adoption requirements, and other topics surrounding adoption.

A.
Relative Adoptions

For adoptions, relatives are defined as blood or adoptive stepparents, grandparents (including great-grandparents), aunts and uncles (including great-uncles and great-aunts), siblings, and first cousins (including first cousins once removed); relatives are also defined as the spouses of these persons.

Relative adoptions typically do not require a home study to be conducted for placement of the adopted child. However, the adoption petition must request that the home study is waived.

B.
Non-Relative Adoptions

Non-relative adoptions are adoptions in which the adoptive parent(s) is not related to the child by blood, adoption, or marriage, and relation, if any, is distant.

These adoptions require a home study before the person or family seeking to adopt may accept the child into their home. A home study is a paid assessment performed by a licensed agency to evaluate the fitness and appropriateness of the prospective adoptive parent or family to adopt.

A home study in Tennessee includes at least one home visit, a criminal background check, a financial fitness assessment, references provided by the prospective adoptive parent(s), a medical evaluation, verification of marital status and age, and interviews with the prospective adoptive parent(s) and household members. A home study ranges from $1,200 to $3,000 in Tennessee and expires after one year.

C.
Uncontested Adoptions and Contested Adoptions

Uncontested adoptions are adoptions in which no one opposes the adoption. The birth parent(s) either consent to the adoption, have had their parental rights terminated, placed the child with an adoption agency, or the child may be in foster care with no available next of kin (parent(s) deceased). In uncontested adoptions, when consent is given by the biological parent(s), the biological parent(s) has only ten days to revoke their consent after executing the adoption documents.

An example of parents consenting to the adoption may be the birth parent(s) agreeing to the grandparents adopting the child or a birth parent agreeing to the other parent's spouse adopting the child.

A birth parent's parental rights may be terminated by agreement of the parent, via a separate dependency and neglect case or if, after proper service of the petition for adoption, there is proof presented at a hearing that there is a basis to terminate the parental rights and proceed with the adoption; the grounds to terminate paternal rights are outlined in Chapter 8.

A contested adoption is any adoption in which one or both of the birth parents are opposing the adoption. In limited circumstances, a relative or someone other than a birth parent may contest an adoption. To grant an adoption of a child over opposition of a parent or both parents, the court must find that there are grounds to terminate parental rights and sever the parent-child relationship.

A biological father who is not married to the child's mother and not listed on the child's birth certificate may execute a Waiver of

Interest, which is immediately irrevocable and prevents the biological father from objecting to or intervening in the child's adoption. The waiver may be signed before the child's birth, but a signed statement, by the mother, naming him as the biological father must be presented to him before he executes the waiver. Where the legal father is not the biological father, such as cases in which the mother is married to someone other than the biological father, the legal father may sign a Denial of Paternity, which is immediately irrevocable and prevents the legal father from objecting to or intervening in the child's adoption.

D.
Requirements and Restrictions in Adoptions

To adopt in Tennessee, there are certain residency requirements for the adopting party, including living or maintaining a residence in Tennessee at the time of the filing for adoption.[73] In all adoptions, an affidavit of financial ability from the petitioner(s) is required to ensure that the adopting person(s) has the financial resources to provide for the child.

Single persons and permitted to adopt. Two unmarried persons cannot adopt the same child. Spouses must adopt jointly, meaning that if you are married and seeking to adopt your spouse must adopt the child as well, unless your spouse is determined to be incompetent by a court. During divorce proceedings, adopted children are addressed in the same manner as biological children; custody/visitation and child support must be addressed if the adoptive children are minors.

Excluding stepparent adoptions, both parents' paternal rights must be terminated during an adoption. Often, one parent will want to terminate the other parent's paternal rights so a relative or friend may adopt the child and share custody of the child with the remaining parent; under Tennessee law, this is not allowed.

---

[73] Exceptions apply for petitioners that have a guardianship order regarding the child from another court in Tennessee, or who are in the military but either resided in Tennessee prior to entering the armed forces or have declared Tennessee their state of legal residency.

Adults may be adopted in Tennessee, and many of the same laws and requirements discussed in this chapter apply to adult adoptions, including termination of biological parents' paternal rights; however, only the consent of the adult being adopted is required and the biological parents have no say so regarding the adult adoption.[74]

In Tennessee, the Tennessee Putative Father Registry and the registry in the birth state of the child, not all states maintain a putative father registry, must be checked in all adoptions.[75] The putative father registry allows an alleged biological father who has no legal relation to a child to register himself and provide information regarding the mother and child so that he may be notified of any adoption proceedings concerning the child.

A form is submitted to the registry within ten days of filing the adoption and the registry returns the form either identifying an alleged biological father or stating that no persons have made claim of being the biological father of the child that is the subject of the adoption proceedings.

Bonus Tidbit: An adoption will terminate any ongoing child support order but has no impact on retroactive child support or child support arrears owed by the parent whose parental rights are terminated. The parent must still pay any retroactive child support or child support arrears owed when the adoption is finalized.

---

[74] The adult being adopted must have the mental capacity to consent to the adoption.
[75] Excluding adult adoptions.

Chapter 8:
Dependency and Neglect

Dependency and neglect proceedings are the legal proceedings in which a parent or legal guardian is accused of abusing and/or neglecting their child. While there are allegations of abuse or neglect, dependency and neglect cases are civil in nature, but separate criminal charges may be brought against a parent or legal guardian depending on the nature or severity of the abuse and/or neglect allegations against them. A finding of dependency and neglect may result in a parent or legal guardian's custodial rights being restricted or removed and may ultimately result in termination of the perpetrator's parental or guardianship rights. Due to the severity of the consequences associated with a finding of dependency and neglect, the burden is high and the child must be dependent and neglected as defined by law. This chapter explores the grounds for dependency and neglect, what happens after a finding of dependency and neglect, and who may file a petition for dependency and neglect. While dependency and neglect may be alleged against a parent or legal guardian, for this chapter, we will focus on when dependency and neglect is alleged against a parent or both parents.

A.
Definition and Grounds for Dependency and Neglect

Tennessee statute defines a "Dependent and Neglected" child as a child:[76]

- Who is without a parent, guardian or legal custodian;
- Whose parent, guardian, or person with whom the child lives, by reason of cruelty, mental incapacity, immorality, or depravity is unfit to properly care for such child;
- Who is under unlawful or improper care, supervision, custody, or restraint by any person, corporation, agency, association, institution, society or other organization, or who is unlawfully kept out of school;
- Whose parent, guardian, or custodian neglects or refuses to provide necessary medical, surgical, institutional, or hospital care for such child;
- Who, because of lack of proper supervision, is found in any place the existence of which violates law;
- Who is in such condition of want or suffering, or is under such improper guardianship or control as to injure or endanger the morals or health of such child or others;

[76] Tennessee Code § 37-1-102 (2021).

- Who is suffering from abuse or neglect;
- Who has been in the care and control of one or more agency or person not related to such child by blood or marriage for a continuous period of six months or longer in the absence of a power of attorney or court order, and such person or agency has not initiated judicial proceedings seeking either legal custody or adoption of the child;
- Who is or has been allowed, encouraged, or permitted to engage in prostitution or obscene or pornographic photographing, filming, posing, or similar activity and whose parent, guardian or other custodian neglects or refuses to protect such child from further such activity; or
- Who has willfully been left in the sole financial care and sole physical care of a related caregiver for not less than eighteen consecutive months by the child's parent, parents, or legal custodian to the related caregiver, and the child will suffer substantial harm if removed from the continuous care of such relative;
- A related caregiver shall include the child's biological, step, or legal grandparent, great-grandparent, sibling, aunt, uncle, or any other person who is legally or biologically related to the child; and
    - A child willfully left with a related caregiver as defined above because of the parent's military service does not constitute dependency and neglect.

A finding of dependency and neglect does not affect a parent's obligation to financially support their child. Until or unless their parental rights are terminated, they should and may be ordered to provide child support for the child(ren).

Bonus Tidbit: For the purposes of dependency and neglect, a related caregiver is not the other parent. If a mother leaves the child with the father for an extended period of time, the father should file for custody not dependency and neglect unless another dependency and neglect ground exist.

B.
Who May File a Petition for Dependency and Neglect?

The other parent, a relative, the Tennessee Department of Children Services, or anyone with knowledge that the child may be dependent and neglected may file the petition. In a dependency and neglect case, the person seeking custody of the child need not be a relative of the child. If the petition is not filed by the Tennessee Department of Children Services then the court must promptly make a referral to the department so that it may investigate. The department will determine if they need to intervene in the case depending upon the findings of the investigation; the department's election not to intervene in a case does not mean that the court will deny the petition or find there are no grounds for dependency and neglect.

Upon filing such a petition, the court has discretion to determine if there is a basis for immediate removal of the child from the accused parent's physical custody based on the allegations in the petition and issue an Ex-Parte Protective Custody Order.[77] If the court issues such an order when the petition is filed, the accused parent(s) is entitled to a preliminary hearing to be set within three judicial days.

---

[77]An emergency and temporary order entered by the court prior to a hearing or any response from the defendant/respondent. Reserved for cases in which there are allegations of irreparable harm to the child unless immediate action is taken by the court.

A finding of dependency and neglect by the court does not mean that the child will be removed from the parent's physical custody, that parental rights will be terminated, that the parent(s) will be prohibited from visiting with the child, or that the parent(s) cannot regain physical custody at a later date. The court's ruling after a finding of dependency and neglect depends on the severity of the abuse and/or neglect and if the cause of the abuse and/or neglect may be readily addressed or eliminated.

In a dependency and neglect case in which the finding of dependency and neglect is only against one parent or the custodial parent is deceased, custody will pass to the other parent unless the other parent is unavailable (i.e., incarcerated, whereabouts unknown, or unwilling to accept custody) or deemed unfit by the court.

Bonus Tidbit: Both legal parents must be given notice of dependency and neglect proceedings even if allegations are not made against both parents.

C.
Reunification

A parent and child may be reunified and/or custody may be returned to the parent(s) after a finding of dependency and neglect, so long as the parent's paternal rights have not been terminated.

If the child has been removed from the parent's or parents' custody after a finding of dependency and neglect, if proper, a permanency plan will be created that establishes requirements for the parent(s) to complete to reunify with the child. A permanency plan is created only in cases involving the Tennessee Department of Children Services when the child or children are to remain in the state's custody. Private dependency and neglect cases will address visitation, if proper, for the parent for which there has been a finding of dependency and neglect against, but there will not be a plan for the parent to regain primary custody. A parent who lost custody due to a finding of dependency and neglect in a case that is not eligible for a permanency plan must file a petition seeking modification of the existing dependency and neglect order with the court if or when they seek to regain primary custody. To regain custody after a finding of dependency and neglect and removal of the child, the petitioner must allege, and the court must find a change in circumstances since entry of the dependency and neglect order; the court must also find that the requested modification is in the best interest of the child.

Here's an example of a case in which I represented a mother in regaining custody after a finding of dependency and neglect:

Mother stipulated to dependency and neglect due to an inability to provide stable housing and for the daily needs of the child. Father failed to participate in the dependency and neglect proceedings, so the child was placed in the custody of a relative; mother was awarded visitation with the child. Over the course of a few years, mother gained and maintained stable employment and housing. Mother also provided financial support to the child's guardian. Mother petitioned the court to modify the order and return custody to her based on the change in her housing and employment circumstances along with the argument that it would be in the child's best interest to be in the custody of mother. The court found that mother's petition was appropriate, that the requirements had been met to return custody to mother and granted mother's petition.

D.
Termination of Parental Rights

According to Tennessee Code § 36-1-113 "Termination of parental or guardianship rights must be based upon:

- A finding by the court of clear and convincing evidence that the grounds for termination of parental or guardianship rights have been established; and
- That termination of the parent's or guardian's rights is in the best interests of the child."

The grounds for termination of parental rights (applies in dependency and neglect cases and adoption cases) are as follows:[78]

- Abandonment by the parent or guardian due to the parent's or guardian's failure to visit, support, or make reasonable payments toward the support of the child for four consecutive months immediately before the filing for the petition to terminate parental rights;
- There has been substantial noncompliance by the parent or guardian with the statement of responsibilities in a permanency plan;
- The child has been removed from the home or the physical or legal custody of a parent or guardian for a period of six months by a court order entered at any stage of proceedings in

[78] Tennessee Code § 36-1-113 (2021).

which a petition has been filed in the juvenile court alleging that a child is a dependent and neglected child, and

- The conditions that led to the child's removal persist, preventing the child's safe return to the care of the parent or guardian, or other conditions exist that, in all reasonable probability, would cause the child to be subjected to further abuse or neglect, preventing the child's safe return to the care of the parent or guardian;
- There is little likelihood these conditions will be remedied at an early date so the child can be safely returned to the parent or guardian in the near future; and
- The continuation of the parent or guardian and child relationship greatly diminishes the child's chances of early integration into a safe, stable, and permanent home;
- The six months must accrue on or before the first date the termination of parental rights petition is set to be heard;

- The parent or guardian has been found to have committed severe child abuse, as defined in Tennessee Code § 37-1-102, under any prior order of a court or is found by the court hearing the petition to terminate parental rights or the petition for adoption to have committed severe child abuse against any child;
- The parent or guardian has been sentenced to more than two years imprisonment for conduct against the child who is the subject of the petition, or for conduct against any sibling or half-sibling of the child or any other child residing temporarily or permanently in the home of such parent or guardian, that has been found under any prior order of a court or that is found by the court hearing the petition to be severe child abuse, as defined in Tennessee Code § 37-1-102. Unless otherwise stated, for purposes of this termination ground, "sentenced" shall not be construed to mean that the

parent or guardian must have served more than two years in confinement, but shall only be construed to mean that the court had imposed a sentence of two or more years upon the parent or guardian;

- The parent has been confined in a correctional or detention facility of any type, by order of the court because of a criminal act, under a sentence of ten or more years, and the child is under eight years of age when the sentence is entered by the court;
- The parent has been:
    - Convicted of first-degree or second-degree murder of the child's other parent or legal guardian; or
    - Found civilly liable for the intentional and wrongful death of the child's other parent or legal guardian;
- The chancery and circuit courts shall have jurisdiction in an adoption proceeding, and the chancery, circuit, and juvenile courts shall have jurisdiction in a separate, independent proceeding conducted before an adoption proceeding to determine if the parent or guardian is mentally incompetent to provide for the further care and supervision of the child, and to terminate that parent's or guardian's rights to the child;
    - The court may terminate the parental or guardianship rights of that parent if it determines based on clear and convincing evidence that:
        - The parent or guardian of the child is incompetent to adequately provide for the further care and supervision of the child because the parent's or guardian's mental condition is presently so impaired and is so likely to remain so that it is unlikely that the parent or guardian will be able to

assume or resume the care of and responsibility for the child in the near future; and

- That termination of parental or guardian rights is in the best interest of the child;
- In the circumstances in the subsections immediately above, no willfulness in the failure of the parent or guardian to establish the parent's or guardian's ability to care for the child needs be shown to establish that the parental or guardianship rights should be terminated;

- The parental rights of any person who, at the time of filing a petition to terminate the parental rights of such person, or if no such petition is filed, at the time of filing a petition to adopt a child, is the presumed father of the child may also be terminated based upon any one or more of these additional grounds:
    - The person has failed, without good cause or excuse, to make reasonable and consistent payments for the support of the child pursuant to the child support guidelines under Tennessee Code § 36-5-101;
    - The person has failed to seek reasonable visitation with the child, and if visitation has been granted, has failed to visit altogether, or has engaged in only token visitation, as defined in Tennessee Code§ 36-1-102;
    - The person has failed to manifest an ability and willingness to assume legal and physical custody of the child;
    - Placing custody of the child in the person's legal and physical custody would pose a risk of substantial harm to the physical or psychological welfare of the child; or

        - The person has failed to file a petition to establish paternity of the child within thirty days after notice of alleged paternity, or as required in Tennessee Code § 36-2-318(j), or after making a claim of paternity under Tennessee Code § 36-1-117(c)(3);
- The parent has been convicted of aggravated rape under Tennessee Code § 39-13-502, rape under Tennessee Code § 39-13-503, or rape of a child under Tennessee Code § 39-13-522, from which crime the child was conceived. A certified copy of the conviction will prove this ground;
    - When one of the child's parents has been convicted of one of the offenses specified above, the child's other parent shall have standing to file a petition to terminate the parental rights of the convicted parent. Nothing in this section shall give a parent standing to file a petition to terminate parental rights based on grounds other than those listed above, the severe sexual child abuse listed below, or attempted first-degree or second-degree murder of the child's other parent or legal guardian;
- The parent has been found to have committed severe child sexual abuse under any prior order of a criminal court;
    - For this section, "severe child sexual abuse" means the parent is convicted of any of the following offenses towards a child:
        - Aggravated rape, under Tennessee Code § 39-13-502;
        - Aggravated sexual battery, under Tennessee Code § 39-13-504;
        - Aggravated sexual exploitation of a minor, under Tennessee Code § 39-17-1004;
        - Especially aggravated sexual exploitation of a minor, under Tennessee Code § 39-17-1005;

    - Incest, under Tennessee Code § 39-15-302;
    - Rape, under Tennessee Code § 39-13-503; or
    - Rape of a child, under Tennessee Code § 39-13-522;
- When one of the child's parents has been convicted of one of the offenses specified above, the child's other parent shall have standing to file a petition to terminate the parental rights of the abusive parent. Nothing in this section shall give a parent standing to file a petition to terminate parental rights based on grounds other than those listed above, the severe sexual child abuse listed below, or attempted first-degree or second-degree murder of the child's other parent or legal guardian;
  - The parent or guardian has been convicted of trafficking for a commercial sex act under § 39-13-309;
  - The parent or guardian has been convicted on or after July 1, 2015, of sex trafficking of children or by force, fraud, or coercion under 18 U.S.C. § 1591, or a sex trafficking of children offense under the laws of another state substantially similar to Tennessee Code § 39-13-309;
  - A parent or guardian has failed to manifest, by act or omission, an ability and willingness to assume legal and physical custody or financial responsibility of the child, and placing the child in the person's legal and physical custody would pose a risk of substantial harm to the physical or psychological welfare of the child; and
  - The parent or legal guardian has been convicted of attempted first-degree murder or attempted second-degree murder of the child's other parent or legal guardian;
    - When one of the child's parents or legal guardians has been convicted of attempted first-degree murder or attempted second-degree murder of the child's other parent

or legal guardian, the child's non-offending parent or legal guardian shall have the standing to file a petition to terminate the parental or guardianship rights of the convicted parent or legal guardian. Nothing in this section shall give a parent or legal guardian standing to file a petition to terminate parental or guardianship rights based on grounds other than those listed above.

Bonus Tidbit: The grounds for dependency and neglect must exist at the time the petition is heard and ruled on by the court. In certain cases, the grounds that existed at the time of filing may have been cured or resolved by the time the petition is heard and ruled upon; dependency and neglect will be denied by the court.

Chapter 9: Grandparent Visitation

Grandparents are often the bedrock of families and are essential in the rearing of children. Because of the close and beneficial relationship between grandparents and grandchildren, Tennessee has established grandparent visitation rights. Grandparent visitation rights are not automatic or absolute; therefore, certain circumstances must exist to trigger grandparent visitation rights. This chapter explains that "grandparent" is legally defined as more than just the parent of one of the child's parents, the circumstances that must exist to qualify for grandparent visitation rights, the factors the court must consider when establishing grandparent visitation, and other important information surrounding grandparent visitation.

A.
Who Qualifies to File a Petition for Grandparent Visitation?

To pursue grandparent visitation, grandparent means but is not limited to biological grandparents, the spouse of a biological grandparent, the parent of an adoptive parent, great-grandparents, and the spouses of great-grandparents.[79] Grandparent visitation is not an automatic right but is available to grandparents if certain circumstances exist.

The court will hear a petition for grandparent visitation only if grandparent visitation is opposed by the custodian or if the grandparent visitation has been severely reduced by the custodian.[80] A grandparent has the legal right to file for grandparent visitation if any of the following apply to their situation:[81]

- The father or mother of an unmarried minor child is deceased;
- The child's father or mother are divorced, legally separated, or were never married to each other;
- The child's father or mother has been missing for not less than six months;
- The court of another state has ordered grandparent visitation;
- The child resided in the home of the grandparent for twelve months or more and was removed from the home by the parent,

---

[79] Tennessee Code § 36-6-306 (2021).
[80] The custodian may be the biological parent(s) or any person with custody.
[81] Tennessee Code § 36-6-306 (2021).

parents, or custodian (this grandparent–grandchild relationship establishes a rebuttable presumption that denial of visitation may cause irreparable harm to the child);[82] or

- The child and the grandparent maintained a significant existing relationship for twelve months or more immediately preceding severance or severe reduction of the relationship, this relationship was severed or severely reduced by the parent, parents, or custodian for reasons other than abuse or presence of a danger of substantial harm to the child, and severance or severe reduction of this relationship is likely to cause substantial emotional harm to the child.

---

[82] The court will assume that the child will suffer severe harm if not allowed to visit with the grandparent unless proof can be given to show otherwise. This harm does not have to be physical, and oftentimes is emotional or psychological.

B.
Factors Considered in a Petition for Grandparent Visitation

In considering a petition for grandparent visitation, Tennessee law requires the court to first determine the presence of a danger of substantial harm to the child if grandparent visitation is not granted. A finding of substantial harm may be based upon termination or severe reduction of the relationship between the minor child and the child's grandparent(s). Tennessee law states there is a presence of substantial harm to the child if any of the following apply, proper proof is required:[83]

- The child had such a significant existing relationship with the grandparent that loss or severe reduction of the relationship is likely to cause severe emotional harm to the child;
- The grandparent functioned as a primary caregiver such that termination or severe reduction of the relationship could adversely affect the daily needs of the child and therefore cause physical or emotional harm to the child; or
- The child had a significant existing relationship with the grandparent and loss or severe reduction of the relationship presents the danger of other direct and substantial harm to the child.
  - A significant relationship exists if the child resided with the grandparent for six consecutive months, the grandparent was the full-time caregiver of the child for at least six consecutive

[83] Tennessee Code § 36-6-306 (2021).

months, or the grandparent frequently visited with the child for at least one year.

There is a rebuttable presumption of substantial harm to the child if the grandparent seeking visitation is the parent of a deceased parent of the minor child(ren) involved in the case.

The court shall also determine if grandparent visitation is in the best interest of the child. The best interest factors are outlined in Tennessee Code § 36-6-307 and are as follows:

- The length and quality of the prior relationship between the child and the grandparent and the role performed by the grandparent;
- The existing emotional ties of the child to the grandparent;
- The preference of the child if the child is determined to be of sufficient maturity to express a preference;
  - The effect of hostility between the grandparent and the parent of the child exhibited in the presence of the child, and the willingness of the grandparent, except if abuse occurs, to encourage a close relationship between the child and the parent(s) or guardian(s) of the child;
  - The good faith of the grandparent in filing the petition;
  - If the parents are divorced or separated, the time-sharing arrangement between the parents regarding the child;
  - If one parent is deceased or missing, that the grandparents requesting visitation are the parents of the deceased or missing person;
  - Any unreasonable deprivation of the grandparent's opportunity to visit with the child by the child's parents or guardian, including denying visitation of the minor child to the grandparent for a period exceeding ninety days;
  - Whether the grandparent is seeking to maintain a significant existing relationship with the child;

- Whether awarding grandparent visitation would interfere with the parent-child relationship; and
- Any court finding that the child's parent or guardian is unfit.

C.
Limitations on Grandparent Visitation

Grandparent visitation is most common where the grandparents' child (mother or father of the minor child) is deceased or otherwise unavailable to visit with the child; unavailability may be due to incarceration, health issues, or substance abuse problems. Grandparents may also pursue grandparent visitation against their own child if their child is attempting to alienate the grandparent after the grandparent raised the grandchild or was the primary caregiver for the grandchild. It is often difficult for a grandparent seeing and visiting with their grandchild through their child to receive court-ordered grandparent visitation; however, it is possible. I had a case in which the father lived out of state and the grandparents lived in Tennessee and had a substantial relationship with the child. The father was awarded parenting time with the child one weekend a month and the grandparents were awarded grandparent visitation with the child one weekend a month.

There is no preset visitation schedule for grandparents, and the schedule is determined case-by-case. There is no concept of "maximum participation" for grandparent visitation. Tennessee cases awarding grandparent visitation have visitation schedules ranging from less than thirty days to a maximum of around eighty days, annually.

Grandparent visitation does not give rise to any other rights, such as rights to school records, medical records, or decision-making authority. Grandparent visitation should never be confused with having joint custody or custodial rights to the child.

About the Author

Attorney Princess M. Woodard is a born, bred, and educated Memphian. Attorney Woodard received her bachelor's degree from Christian Brothers University and her law degree from the University of Memphis. Attorney Woodard has been in the legal field for more than a decade, a licensed Tennessee attorney since 2015, and a certified family law mediator since 2018. Her practice is concentrated in domestic relations law and she has handled hundreds of family law cases, both simple and complex. Attorney Woodard is a true litigator with extensive trial experience and victories before the Tennessee Court of Appeals.

Attorney Woodard's professional talent is reflected in the honors and accolades she's received, including being named an 'Attorney for Justice' by the Tennessee Supreme Court, the 'Best of the Bar' by the Memphis Business Journal, 'Outstanding Associate of the Year' by the Memphis Chapter of the American Inns of Court, and being selected as one of only three family law attorneys from across the country to serve a 2021-2023 Family Law Fellow by the American Bar Association.

Attorney Woodard's clients have described her as "a beast, and she's the best," "the type of lawyer you should want to keep on speed dial," and "an attorney who's going to fight for you and your rights."

Attorney Woodard is very involved in her community as a member of numerous professional, community, and service organizations. Attorney Woodard's legal practice is located in Memphis, Tennessee.

To learn more or contact Attorney Woodard, please visit www.woodardesq.com.

www.ingramcontent.com/pod-product-compliance
Lightning Source LLC
LaVergne TN
LVHW040515210926
848480LV00005BA/1472
9781733562263